COMMON
WILD FLOW
& PLANT
of NOVA SCOTIA

NIMBUS
PUBLISHING

NOVA SCOTIA
Transportation and Public Works

Nimbus Publishing Limited
PO Box 9166, Halifax, NS   B3K 5M8
(902) 455-4286

Printed and bound in Canada
Design: Kathy Kaulbach, Paragon Design Group

National Library of Canada Cataloguing in Publication

LaRue, Diane, 1943–
Common wild flowers & plants of Nova Scotia / Diane LaRue.
Co-published by the Nova Scotia Dept. of Transportation and Public Works.
ISBN 1-55109-488-6

1. Wild flowers—Nova Scotia—Identification. 2. Plants—Nova Scotia—Identification. 3. Roadside plants—Nova Scotia. 4. Natural landscaping—Nova Scotia. I. Nova Scotia. Dept. of Transportation and Public Works II. Title. III. Title: Wild flowers & plants. IV. Title: Common wild flowers and plants of Nova Scotia.
QK203.N6L37 2004   580'.9716   C2004-902490-6

Canada

The Canada Council | Le Conseil des Arts
for the Arts | du Canada

We acknowledge the financial support of the Government of Canada through the Book Publishing Industry Development Program (BPIDP) and the Canada Council for our publishing activities.

Disclaimer

The information provided in this book is intended as a general guide in the identification, appreciation, and use of native and naturalized plants. The author holds no responsibility for any usage of plants mentioned in this book. The author does not condone the digging of plant material from the wild, except in areas doomed to destruction and then only with landowner permission.

TABLE OF CONTENTS

SHRUBS

GRASSES & GRASS-LIKE PLANTS

FERNS & FERN ALLIES

LICHENS & BRYOPHYTES

UNDESIRABLE PLANTS

RESTORATION TECHNIQUES

ACKNOWLEDGMENTS

This book is the result of the vision, excitement, encouragement, and support of many people. Key people who have wholeheartedly supported me in every way in my love for Nova Scotia's plant species and communities have been Denis Rushton, Christene Almon of Environmental Services, Nova Scotia Department of Transportation and Public Works, and Jeff Morton, Nova Scotia Agricultural College. I am grateful to each of them for their enthusiasm and continual encouragement.

The basis of the book rests upon knowledge gained through my years of working with roadside vegetation, during which time I became fascinated with Nova Scotia's native plants and plant communities and how they survive and thrive, particularly through human disruptions in land use. I thank the Government of Canada and the Government of Nova Scotia for their bilateral agreements, which provided funding for research projects on the many aspects of roadside vegetation and its management. I am grateful to the partnership institutions that provided the infrastructure for me to carry out this work: Nova Scotia Department of Transportation and Public Works (NSTPW), Nova Scotia Agricultural College (NSAC) and Nova Scotia Department of Agriculture and Fisheries (NSDAF) (formerly Department of Agriculture and Marketing).

I thank Marian Munro (Nova Scotia Museum of Natural History), Rick Hoeg (NSDAF), Mike Crowell, and members of the Halifax Field Naturalists for so readily identifying plants for me. I am very thankful for the part-time student assistance I have received over the years and for the significant contribution made by Belinda Culgin in the final stages of preparation for NSDTPW's *Integrated Roadside Vegetation Management Manual* and the *Roadside Vegetation Field Manual*, from which this book was born. I am grateful to Kathy Kaulbach, Paragon Design Group, for her illustrations and guidance, and for the passion she puts into her work. Thank you to Carolyn Terry and Sandra Fisk (NSAC) for their talents, which freed me to carry out the tasks I am good at. Thank you also to June Hall for her valuable comments and editing. I am also grateful for the office space and work environment provided by Tom Gouthro (Technical Services, NSDTPW). A special thanks to the many people in NSDTPW's highway operations who provided encouragement and information on how roadside plant communities can be managed ecologically in a sustainable manner.

Special acknowledgment goes to the Nova Scotia Museum of Natural History for the wealth of ecological, soil, plant, and habitat information provided in the *Natural History of Nova Scotia, Volumes I* and *II*. Marian Zinck's *Roland's Flora of Nova Scotia, Volumes I* and *II*, and Ray Fielding's *Shrubs of Nova Scotia* have been valuable for species' nomenclature, plant descriptions, and ecology.

Diane LaRue
Halifax, Nova Scotia, January 2004

NOVA SCOTIA IS A BEAUTIFUL PROVINCE and we are blessed with a diversity of beautiful native lichens, mosses, grasses, wild flowers, shrubs, and trees, along with many naturalized species that were either brought intentionally by early Europeans for medicinal, culinary, and livestock use, or else are unintentional introductions. On some sites only native species are found. On others, there is a blend of native and naturalized species. These diverse plant communities are adapted to Nova Scotia's climate and soils.

The selection of the 100 or so species in this handbook is based on plants commonly found on roadsides and other sunny locations in Nova Scotia. Also included are typical wet-land species found in roadside ditches.

Many of these sunny habitats are highly disturbed, the sort of environment where weedy species, many of them introduced, will thrive. With time, however, native wildflowers, shrubs, and trees move in, returning the site to the wild. This book, there-fore, includes both native and introduced species. What it does not include are large trees, or the plants of Nova Scotia's shady woodlands.

In addition to plants with landscape value, the handbook cov-ers undesirable plants. These are plants classified as noxious under Nova Scotia's Weed Control Act, or of ecological concern, or that are particularly invasive. These are covered in a separate section.

In the section on restoration techniques, a variety of vegetation establishment and management techniques is presented in the form of fact sheets. These fact sheets are intended to present the information in an attractive, easily readable form and to be useful for vegetation managers, reclamation and restoration project managers, landscapers, and homeowners who wish to utilize native plants and communities on their properties. They are based on an understanding of the ecological concepts important for establishing and enhancing a desired vegetative cover. The techniques cover seeding from seed mixes and wild-flowers, shrub propagation, and soil improvement.

This handbook is designed to be a usable reference that can be taken out into the field. It is hoped that it will help to engender excitement over Nova Scotia's plant communities and to foster an appreciation of the need to conserve native ecosystems.

ABOUT PLANT NAMES

The way to correctly identify a plant is by its botanical or scientific name, rather than its common name. The botanical name has two parts, which are typically italicized. The first, the *genus name*, represents a group of plants within a family of related plants and is always capitalized. The second, the *species name*, indicates the particular type of plant; the first letter of the species is usually not capitalized. Names and initials following the scientific name refer to the person who named the plant. Common names for the same species of plant often differ from place to place and by use, and are considered less reliable for identification. All scientific names and most common names used in this book are taken from *Roland's Flora of Nova Scotia*, revised by Marian Zinck (1998, Nova Scotia Museum and Nimbus Publishing). This two-volume book provides keys for identifying plants, and covers the 136 families of vascular plants found in Nova Scotia.

In this book a number of terms are used to describe species. *Native* refers to plants that existed in Nova Scotia prior to European settlement. Most *introduced* plants originated somewhere in Eurasia, and were brought here either intentionally or unintentionally. Some of the medicinal and culinary herbs brought by European immigrants have been adapted into use by other population groups in Nova Scotia. *Naturalized* refers to those introduced species that like the growing conditions here and have taken up residence by readily reproducing when conditions are right. *Invasive* refers to those introduced species that thrive so well here that they are replacing native plant species; by doing so, they decrease habitat and biodiversity.

WILDFLOWERS

ANNUAL CLOVERS

[ABOVE] *Rabbitfoot Clover, Hop Clover and Wild Chamomile*

[RIGHT]
Hop Clover

CLOVERS are recognized by their three oval leaflets and small flowers arranged in heads or spikes. A number of species of annual and perennial clovers thrive in Nova Scotia. Some are grown as agricultural crops and others exist in natural settings; none of them is native. The two most common species of annual clover along roadsides are Rabbitfoot Clover and Hop Clover.

HOP CLOVER (*T. campestre*) is a small, dainty, annual plant less than 40 cm tall. Its three oval leaflets are slightly notched, and the middle leaflet has a longer stalk than the other two. The yellow flowers are also oval shaped, as is typical of clovers. Like other clovers, Hop Clover has the ability to take nitrogen from the air through *Rhizobium* fixation. These bacteria induce the plant to form nodules on its roots. Reproduction is by seed.

RABBITFOOT CLOVER (*T. arvense*) is a small, erect, annual plant that is freely branching, has dense, hairy stems and narrow leaves, and grows less than 40 cm tall. When mature the stems are often reddish. The flowers provide a soft, fuzzy, pinkish-grey glow along roadside shoulders and are often seen with the yellow flower of Hop Clover, blooming from July to September. This clover gained its name from its fuzzy flower, which resembles a rabbit's foot. An annual, it reproduces by seed. The roots consist of a taproot with a secondary fibrous root system that allows it to thrive in variable moisture conditions.

Family: Fabaceae or Pea Family

HABITAT

Prefer sun to part shade.

Both these annual clovers are found on nutrient-deficient soils that are sandy or dry and rocky.

Form colonies along gravel shoulders of roads and in waste places and old fields.

GENERAL COMMENTS:

These clovers are desirable ground covers, providing neat, low-growing flowering carpets. As nitrogen fixers they help enrich poor-quality soils while providing a beautiful, soft pink-and-yellow tinge to the landscape.

Rabbitfoot Clover

ASTERS

There are 18 species of perennial asters in Nova Scotia, and they all bloom in mid- to late summer. The two most common species with violet-blue flower heads seen on our roadsides are NEW YORK ASTER (*Aster novi-belgii*) and NEW ENGLAND ASTER (*Aster novae-angliae*), which readily form hybrids. New York Aster is more commonly seen along roadsides. Most New England and New York Asters have deep-violet flowers but there are variations from blue to violet. Another common species is Tall White Aster, which is described on p. 42.

Both New York Aster and New England Aster are stout plants that grow to 1 m or less. The leaves can vary in width but are generally narrow and lance shaped. The stem can be hairy (New England Aster) to smooth (New York Aster) but variation occurs with hybridization. The violet colour of the flowers is quite noticeable along roadsides from July to October. Identification is difficult and mature plants with flowers are needed for identification.

Family: Asteraceae or Aster Family

Prefer sunny conditions.

Thrive in dry to moist soils.

Usually found along roadsides, and in swamps and meadows.

Tolerant of salt conditions and found along seashores.

General Comments

The violet-blue flowers of these native asters are a welcome addition to the late-summer and fall colours of Nova Scotia's roadsides and waste places, and provide a showy display in gardens.

Galium spp.

There are a dozen species of Galium in Nova Scotia. They can be identified by their square, slender stems, their whorls of leaves, and their small, white flowers.

CLEAVERS (*Galium aparine* and *Galium mollugo*) are our most common species of *Galium*—sprawling plants with oblong leaves in whorls of six to eight whose white flowers are held in branched clusters at the stem ends. Cleavers have rough hairs on their leaves, downward-pointing hairs on the stem corners, and fruit covered with bristles. These hairs are very clingy and stick to clothing. The small, recurved prickles also allow the plant to cling to other plants.

Bedstraws are distinguished by their hairless leaves. Species that are common throughout Nova Scotia include Common Bedstraw (*Galium palustre*), Rough Bedstraw (*Galium asprellum*), and Small Bedstraw (*Galium tinctorium*).

Family: Rubiaceae or Madder Family

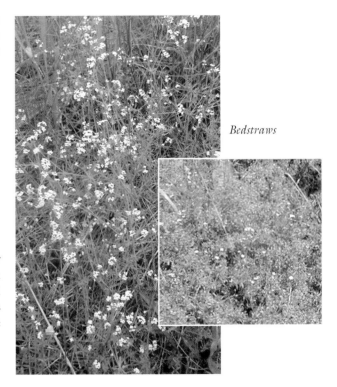

Bedstraws

Habitat

Prefer shade to part shade.
Prefer nutrient-rich, organic soils.
Usually found along roadsides and in fields.

General Comments

Cleavers grow on elongated stems that are notorious for their ability to cling to other plants, clothing or animals. They can form a dense mat. Cleavers have been collected as medicinal plants. Some bedstraws contain sweet-smelling compounds and were traditionally used to stuff mattresses, hence the common name.

BITTERSWEET or NIGHTSHADE

There are 1500 named species of NIGHTSHADE but only three are found in Nova Scotia. All three are introduced species. BITTERSWEET is a distinctive perennial vine with hairy, oval, alternate leaves. Its stem is woody at the base and slightly hairy. The purple-blue flowers with yellow centres resemble those of a potato, a close relative, and can be seen blooming from mid-May to September. The oval berries are bright red and quite poisonous, even toxic when not ripe.

Family: Solanaceae or Nightshade Family

HABITAT

Prefers sun to part shade.

Thrives in moist soil.

Usually found on roadsides, wastplaces, and along the edges of cultivated fields and wooded areas.

GENERAL COMMENTS

Bittersweet is becoming a serious weed in some areas. It should also be discouraged since the bright-red berries are TOXIC and sometimes mistaken for edible fruit.

BIRDSFOOT-TREFOIL

BIRDSFOOT-TREFOIL is an introduced perennial with many stems and a low-to-prostrate growth habit up to 60 cm high. The leaves are divided into five oblong leaflets. Bright-yellow flowers are carried in branched clusters on umbels, and bloom from July to September, making a colourful showing on roadsides. The fruit are arranged in pods that look like a bird's foot. Reproduction is by seeds and also by rhizomes and stolons.

Family: Fabaceae or Pea Family

HABITAT

Prefers full sun.
Grows on a wide variety of soil types, including gravel.
Adaptable to various moisture regimes, including drought.
Usually found on roadsides and in old fields, meadows, and
waste places.

GENERAL COMMENTS

As a member of the legume family, Birdsfoot-trefoil is able to fix atmospheric nitrogen and is therefore used not only for its beautiful, long-lasting yellow blooms, but also for its ability to improve soil fertility. In addition, its coarse secondary root system makes it a useful plant for soil stabilization. It may be slow to establish, but makes a good ground cover in unmowed areas when mixed with grasses.

BLACK-EYED SUSAN

BLACK-EYED SUSAN is a beautiful perennial found in many areas of Nova Scotia. Although not native to the province, it is a North American species. The plants are coarse, rough, and hairy. Its stem has few or no branches, and its leaves are lance shaped and without teeth. The flowers are in showy, solitary heads, each of which has 10 to 20 golden-orange ray florets and a brown, cone-shaped centre. Blooming begins in mid-July and persists well into September.

Family: Asteraceae or Aster family

HABITAT

Thrives in full sun.
Tolerant of different soils, including sandy, acidic, low-fertility soils, as well as clay soils with higher pHs.
Found in old fields, waste places, and roadsides.

Patches of Black-eyed Susan can be seen along several stretches of Nova Scotia's highways. In plant communities on sandy soils it is found associated with Sweetfern; on other sites it is found in community with roadside wildflowers such as Ox-eye Daisy, Goldenrod, and Aster. With its colourful, long-lasting blooms, Black-eyed Susan is a highly desirable wildflower.

This native of North America's prairie habitats has a fibrous root system that provides a large area for water uptake, so the plant is well adapted to dry conditions. Black-eyed Susan can be used along with Ox-eye Daisy for landscape beautification in naturalized meadows or grassy plantings. Continued mowing will discourage it, so mowing should take place after flowering and seed dispersal. Reproduction is by seed, and not vegetatively by roots.

BLUE FLAG

BLUE FLAG is a graceful, sword-leaved plant that is 50 to 80 cm tall. The violet flowers are boldly veined, have down-curved petals, and bloom in June and July. It is a native plant, found from Labrador to Manitoba, south to West Virginia and Minnesota. This plant is a monocot, but is included here because of its beautiful flowers.

Family: Iridaceae or Iris Family

HABITAT

Prefers sun to partial shade.

Requires moist, bog-type soils.

Commonly found in meadows, swamps, and roadside ditches, and alongside streams.

GENERAL COMMENTS

Blue Flag makes a beautiful showing in roadside ditches, water gardens, along the edges of ponds, and in other moist areas, where it may naturalize. It likes a rich soil with ample organic material. A rhizomatous plant, it can be propagated either by seed or by cutting individual corms or bulbs off the mother plant and transplanting them.

BLUETS is the only species of *Hedyotis* in Nova Scotia. Its small, four-parted, white to pale-blue flowers have a bright yellow eye, and bloom from mid-May to mid-June. The leaves are in clusters at the base and scattered on the stem. This native plant is common throughout Nova Scotia, particularly in the Halifax Regional Municipality.

Family: Rubiaceae or Madder family

HABITAT

Prefers sun to part shade.
Commonly found on moist, acid soil.
Usually growing on hillsides, roadsides, and grassy pastures.

GENERAL COMMENTS

This small, delicate plant makes a beautiful showing on roadsides and is a welcome addition to grassy areas and gardens. It comes alive in early spring with hundreds (on a mature plant) of little pale-blue to white flowers that seem to glow. It grows no more than a few centimetres high.

BONESET

BONESET is a native perennial, one of four *Eupatorium* species growing in Nova Scotia. This tall, erect plant grows to 1.5 m. Its leaves are rough, veined, wrinkled on both surfaces—and arranged opposite each other on the stem so that the rough, hairy stem appears to grow through the centre of the leaves. In August and September numerous branched clusters of whitish flower heads are borne on stems arising from the leaf nodes.

Family: Asteraceae or Aster Family

HABITAT

Prefers sun to part shade.

Thrives in moist soils.

Found in wet meadows, bogs, and roadside ditches, and at the edges of swamps and streams.

GENERAL COMMENTS

The unusual foliage and clusters of white flowers make this an attractive plant in sunny locations with moist soils. Boneset was historically used to cure ailments such as influenza and fevers.

CANADA THISTLE is a hairless, much-branched perennial that grows to over 1 m in height, bears male and female flowers on different plants (the only thistle to do so), and spreads by both seeds and rhizomes. Its deeply lobed leaves are quite prickly. Canada Thistle blooms from July to August, bearing numerous small purplish-pink flower heads.

Family: Asteraceae or Aster Family

HABITAT

Prefers full sun.
Tolerates a variety of soil and moisture conditions.
Usually grows in fields, roadsides, waste ground and
pastures. Occasionally found as individuals on
roadsides, but more often in patches on back slopes.

GENERAL COMMENTS

This serious agricultural weed, which was introduced from Europe, is one of the most common thistles in the province. It is prickly and spreads rapidly from roots. Patches found on roadsides often maintain populations of biological control agents.

CINQUEFOIL or FIVE-FINGER

Potentilla simplex Michx.

CINQUEFOIL or FIVE-FINGER is a trailing perennial plant, native to Nova Scotia, that is common on roadsides and waste places. Its long runners root at the nodes, forming new crowns from which the long-stalked leaves, solitary yellow flowers and new runners arise. The leaves are divided into five leaflets (or more), hence the name Five-finger. This plant is native to eastern and central North America and is found throughout Nova Scotia.

Family: Rosaceae or Rose Family

HABITAT

Thrives in full sun.

Prefers well-drained, moderate soil.

Usually found in dry, open woods, old fields, and waste places, and on grassy hillsides and roadsides.

GENERAL COMMENTS

Cinquefoil establishes easily in poor soils and on bark mulches, where it forms a dense, ground-hugging cover with yellow flowers. It often is found with Wild Strawberry, another native ground cover, providing a delightful combination of yellow and white flowers.

COMMON MULLEIN is often seen blooming along roadsides from late June to September. It is tall, reaching 2 m, with a club-like spike of yellow five-petaled flowers at the top of the stem. The plant has a flannel-like coating over its leaves and stem, and has oblong, lance-shaped leaves that are widest above the middle and have a sharp tip.

Family: Scrophulariaceae or Snapdragon Family

HABITAT

Prefers sun.
Thrives in light, dry gravel or stony soils.
Usually found on roadsides, hillsides, and pastures.

GENERAL COMMENTS

Mullein was introduced from Europe as a medicinal herb and has naturalized along roadsides and in waste places. This tall, stately, sturdy plant, with its woolly stems and foliage and its yellow flowers, provides a spectacular show.

CROWN VETCH

CROWN VETCH is commonly seeded on roadsides elsewhere in North America, including Ontario, for the dense vegetative cover and erosion control is provides, but is rarely found on Nova Scotia roadsides. This introduced perennial from Europe has a reclining growth habit, its creeping stems reaching several metres in length. The leaves have numerous leaflets. In July Crown Vetch is covered with masses of beautiful pink flowers.

Family: Fabaceae or Pea Family

HABITAT

Thrives in full sun.
Prefers poor, nutrient-deficient soils.
Usually grows on embankments and along roadsides.

GENERAL COMMENTS

This nitrogen-fixing, low-growing plant forms a dense vegetative cover and is useful in erosion control. When established, however, it crowds out other plants, and in some areas of North America is considered invasive and difficult to control because of its seeding ability and rapid spread.

CURLY DOCK

CURLY DOCK (YELLOW DOCK, CURLED DOCK) is a taprooted perennial with a basal rosette of wavy, oval leaves and a flower stem up to 1 m in height. Introduced from Europe, Curly Dock is now widely naturalized throughout temperate North America. The large, deep taproot allows the plant to survive during periods of low moisture. The large oval leaves are bright green in spring, but in summer and fall they may take on a reddish-purple tinge.

Family: Polygonaceae or Buckwheat Family

HABITAT

Prefers sun to part shade.
Thrives on nutrient-rich, heavy, damp soils but does not tolerate cultivation.
Usually found on roadsides, meadows, pastures, drainage ditches, and waste areas.

GENERAL COMMENTS

Curly Dock is generally considered a troublesome or even noxious weed throughout North America, except where it is used as an edible green or a medicinal plant, but its reddish-brown seeds and flower stalks spiking upwards provide a distinctive visual appearance in late summer, fall, and winter along our roadsides.

DAISY FLEABANES resemble asters but they bloom a little earlier—from June to September. The ray florets have narrow white petals that occasionally have a pink or blue tinge. The plant is a biennial, with a rosette of leaves in the first year and a flower stalk (to 1 m) in the second. The leaves are wide, hairy, lance shaped, and slightly toothed.

Family: Asteraceae or Aster Family

HABITAT

Prefers sun.
Usually grows in sandy, disturbed soils.
Found on roadsides, neglected fields,
and waste ground.

GENERAL COMMENTS

The two Daisy Fleabane species in Nova Scotia (*Erigeron annus* and *E. strigosu*s) are generally considered to be weeds, but their bright, prolific flowers provide a welcome show of white. They resemble Ox-eye Daisy, but the flower heads are only half the diameter and have two to four times as many ray florets. The common name comes from an old belief that they repel fleas and other pestiferous insects. The belief persisted for generations, even though Daisy Fleabanes appear to have no insect-repelling ability.

DEPTFORD PINK

DEPTFORD PINK is a native of Europe but widely naturalized in North America. This annual or biennial grows from 15 to 50 cm tall. The small pink flowers are borne in small, flat, terminal clusters, and bloom from May to June. The leaves are long and narrow or lance shaped. Deptford Pink is predominantly found in southern Nova Scotia but is scattered throughout the province.

Family: Caryophyllaceae or Pink Family

HABITAT

Prefers sun.
Thrives in well-drained soil.
Usually grows in dry fields and on roadsides.

GENERAL COMMENTS

Although common along roadsides in unmowed areas, this is an inconspicuous plant, rarely visible to the passing motorist. It thrives along with various grasses and provides a pleasant show in amongst other flowers or in a grassy setting.

EVENING-PRIMROSE

EVENING-PRIMROSE is a native wildflower, widespread throughout Canada and the United States, that is 60 to 80 cm tall. The large, yellow flowers have four petals atop a long floral tube, and bloom from July to September. The fruit is a hairy oblong capsule that easily shatters to scatter seeds.

Evening-primrose is a biennial with a large fleshy taproot. In the first year it produces a flat-lying rosette; in the second it elongates, becoming coarse and woody. A related species, Small-flowered Evening-primrose *(O. parviflora)*, is similar, but its petals are small and linear.

Family: Onagraceae or Evening-primrose Family

HABITAT

Prefers full sun.
Thrives in dry, open soil and tolerates a range of PH..
Generally found in fields and along roadsides.

GENERAL COMMENTS

The scented, showy flowers open at dusk so that they can be pollinated by night-time insects, and close by noon. The entire plant is edible and the seeds, leaves, and root are used medicinally. It is grown commercially in Nova Scotia for its seed oil, which is rich in unsaturated fatty acids.

FIREWEED is a tall (1–2 m), robust, native perennial found throughout Canada. Its long, slender leaves are alternate on the stem, its showy pink flowers held on a long pyramidal spike. The flowers, which bloom from early July to August, are an important source of nectar for honeybees. Each flower produces a seed capsule containing 300 to 500 seeds, which have tufts of white, fuzzy hairs on one end. Fireweed rapidly establishes through airborne seeds and spreads through rhizomes and fine roots that may extend 45 cm into soil. Seeds require bare mineral soil and high light for germination.

Family: Onagraceae or Evening-primrose Family

HABITAT

Prefers sunny areas.

Thrives in clays, through sandy loam, to unweathered parent material. Prefers a soil pH over 5.

Quickly establishes in burnt-over areas, and also found along fence rows, waste places, and on roadsides.

GENERAL COMMENTS

This colourful native perennial plant dominates many plant communities undergoing succession, quickly reclaiming disturbed ground. Also commonly known as Rosebay Willowherb and Great Willowherb, Fireweed has a long history of use as both a food and a medicinal, and is useful in revegetating disturbed areas.

GOAT'S-BEARD or SALSIFY is an introduced biennial from Europe and a common sight throughout the province. Its foliage is grasslike, forming a basal rosette the first year. The plant becomes erect in the second year, reaching 30 to 60 cm. Salsify's yellow flowers (or more properly, flower heads) are borne singly at the ends of unbranched stems. Notably, the pointed, greenish bracts are longer than the yellow rays. Salsify produces a milky sap and has a fleshy taproot.

Family: Asteraceae or Aster Family

HABITAT

Prefers full sun.
Thrives in dry, open, disturbed soil.
Usually found on waste ground, roadsides, and grassland.

GENERAL COMMENTS

Often considered a weed, this handsome plant is a close relation of the hawkweeds. Goat's-beard opens its blossoms in the morning and closes them before noon, except in cloudy weather. When the flower goes to seed it resembles a giant dandelion. The beautiful feathery down on each seed is the means by which the seeds are wafted by the wind and freely scattered. The yellow flower balls are used in floral arrangements.

GOLDENRODS

There are 19 species of GOLDENROD (16 *Solidago* and 3 *Euthamia*) in Nova Scotia. All are native and all flower in late summer. These perennial plants have an erect growth habit and minimal branching. Their leaves are simple and alternate on the stems. Except for *S. bicolor*, which has white flowers, all goldenrods have yellow flowers. Most species are typically found in open, sunny, or partially sunny habitats. All reproduce by both seed and rhizomes, and many readily form clumps of genetically identical stems. Goldenrods provide a substantial part of the herbaceous flora that blooms in the late summer and fall in our province, and are an important group to know.

Goldenrods are notoriously difficult to identify, and many hybridize, making the task even more difficult. Older identification keys placed them in one of five groups based on shape: plume-like, elm-branched, club-like or showy, wand-like, and flat topped. A second way to identify goldenrods is through the many insects that lay their eggs in different species, which then produce galls. Knowing which insect prefers which species of goldenrod makes the process of identification much easier.

Some commonly seen species:

CANADA GOLDENROD or TALL GOLDENROD, *Solidago canadensis*, is an example of the plume-like shape. This very common goldenrod grows to 1.5 m and frequently invades areas of poor soils such as the poorly vegetated back slopes of roadsides and along the edges of fields. The leaves are toothed, rough textured, and parallel veined.

ROUGH-STEMMED GOLDENROD, *S. rugosa*, grows to 1.6 m and is also found on roadsides and abandoned fields. It is an example of the elm-branched shape. The leaves are deeply toothed and feather veined.

The gorgeous SEASIDE GOLDENROD, *S. sempervirens*, has thick, fleshy leaves that help conserve moisture in coastal and salt-marsh habitats. The heavy, plume-like inflorescence exudes a rich, goldenrod fragrance.

LANCE-LEAVED GOLDENROD, *Euthamia graminifolia*, is a common flat-topped goldenrod. It has long, thin leaves with three to five veins, can grow to 1.5 m tall, and likes moist, sunny places. SLENDER FRAGRANT GOLDENROD, *E. tenuifolia*, is similar, with narrower leaves and a single vein.

Family: Asteraceae or Aster Family

Prefer full sun.
Tolerate variable soil conditions but prefer dry, open areas.
Found in meadows, old fields, woods,
   salt marshes, and on roadsides and seashores.

GENERAL COMMENTS

Masses of bright-yellow goldenrod flowers are a delight to
the eye, wherever they grow. They are a dominant part of our
late-summer and fall landscape. In addition to their glorious
colour, they have been valued by herbalists for centuries, and
are used to make yellow dyes. The flowers are an important
source of nectar to honeybees.

Goldenrods are NOT responsible for hay fever! The flowers
are brightly coloured to attract insect pollinators and there-
fore hold onto their pollen, which is large and sticky. Plants
with drab flowers, such as Ragweed, are wind-pollinated and
have no need to attract insects. But goldenrods and Ragweed
bloom at the same time, and guess who gets the blame.

*A field of goldenrod
and Pearly Everlasting*

About a dozen species of HAWKWEEDS grow in Nova Scotia, most of them introduced from Europe. Hawkweeds are perennials with alternate or basal leaves. Their stems exude a milky sap when broken. The bright-yellow to orange flowers can be seen along roadsides from June to August. Species commonly seen on our roadsides as part of shoulder and back-slope communities include:

ORANGE HAWKWEED or DEVIL'S PAINTBRUSH (*Hieracium aurantiacum*) grows 10 to 60 cm tall in leached and well-drained soils or slopes, including old fields. With flower heads that are bright reddish orange, it is the only species of hawkweed without yellow flowers. Patches are quite noticeable when the plant blooms in June through August.

Hieracium lachenalii can reach heights up to 1 m. Its leaves are blotched with purple and usually grow in a basal rosette. The branches are woolly. Yellow flowers bloom in July and August.

KING DEVIL HAWKWEED (*Hieracium piloselloides*) is our tallest species, growing from 20 to 100 cm tall. Conspicuous along roadsides, it forms large patches with bright-yellow flowers in June and July. It is also common in fields, pastures, and waste places.

MOUSE-EARED HAWKWEED (*Hieracium pilosella*) is a low-growing species found in pastures and shady areas. It is common on roadsides, especially on poorly grassed or bare slopes. The yellow flower heads, which look a lot like dandelions, are borne on leafless, hairy stems, providing a colourful display from mid-June to early August. The leaves are hairy and lance shaped.

Family: Asteraceae or Aster Family

HABITAT

Prefer full sun.
Thrive in poor, dry, sandy, gravel soils with
  low fertility and low pH.
Usually found in fields and ditches, and on
  roadsides and banks.

GENERAL COMMENTS

Although of a weedy nature, hawkweeds provide a showy display of colour when massed in bunches. They are able to colonize and dominate new sites of bare soil because of their tolerance for low-productivity soil and a range of successful reproductive strategies: seeds, rhizomes, stolons, and adventitious roots. Some hawkweeds are considered highly invasive in North America. Once established, they quickly develop into patches that continue to expand until covering the site with a solid mat of rosettes.

[RIGHT]
*King Devil
Hawkweed*

[BACKGROUND]
*Hieracium
lachenalii*

JOE-PYE-WEED

JOE-PYE-WEED is a striking native perennial, up to 2 m tall, that forms large, colourful colonies on wet soils. Its generally unbranched stem is mottled with purple amd its lance-shaped leaves arise from the nodes in whorls of three to five. Joe-pye-weed blooms from July to September, with pinkish-lavender to purple flower heads massed in branched, flat-topped clusters 5 to 20 cm wide.

Family: Asteraceae or Aster Family

HABITAT

Prefers sun to part shade.

Thrives in moist soils.

Found on the edges of meadows, alongside brooke, and in wet thickets and ditches.

GENERAL COMMENTS

Few perennials can compare with Joe-pye-weed's ability to create an impressive presence in the natural landscape. The large terminal clusters of pinkish-purple flowers appear in late summer in roadside ditches, in meadows and swamps. Joe-pye-weed gained its name from a medicine man named Joe Pye, who was said to have cured typhus using the plant.

KNAPWEED

KNAPWEED is an introduced perennial that spreads by seed and is becoming quite weedy on our roadsides. This species is the most common of four knapweeds in Nova Scotia. Its stems are branched and somewhat woody, its leaves lobed in various ways. The purple flower heads bloom from July to September. Knapweed is 20 to 80 cm tall and is becoming more common in many areas with reduced roadside mowing.

Family: Asteraceae or Aster Family

HABITAT

Thrives in sun.
Prefers dry, infertile soils, but adapts to many types of soil.
Usually found along roadsides and on waste
   ground and pastures.

GENERAL COMMENTS

Knapweed can be a problem weed in agriculture and gardens and on roadsides. Its vibrant purple flowers are attractive but its thick woody growth and extensive root system allow it to dominate sites and crowd out other, more desirable plants.

LUPINE

LUPINE is a perennial growing up to 1 m tall that was introduced to Nova Scotia from western North America. Lupines are now found from Nova Scotia to Ontario and south to New England, and from Alaska to California. Their soft, fan-shaped leaves are divided into small, finger-like leaflets, eight to 16 in number. Lupines have beautiful long spikes of pea-shaped flowers coloured white, pink, or a clear azure blue. Masses of these showy flowers dot our roadsides from late June to early July.

Family: Fabaceae or Pea Family

HABITAT

Prefers sun to part shade.
Tolerant of different soils.
Usually found along roadsides, and in fields and meadows.

GENERAL COMMENTS

Lupines provide a showy mass of colour when in bloom. They colonize poor soils and spread on their own through seed production.

OX-EYE DAISY

OX-EYE DAISY or COMMON WHITE DAISY is an abundant plant in Nova Scotia's fields and meadows. Introduced from Europe by early settlers and now thoroughly naturalized, this daisy spreads by seeds and shallow, slowly extending rootstocks. Ox-eye Daisy is a multi-stemmed plant growing 20 to 30 cm high. The basal leaves are deeply lobed; those higher up the stems are long and narrow. The flower heads are 4 to 5 cm across, have pure-white ray florets and a yellow centre, and are borne individually on long, naked stalks.

Family: Asteraceae or Aster Family

HABITAT

Prefers full sun.
Thrives in well-drained soils.
Usually found in cultivated fields, pastures, roadsides,
    waste areas and along railway lines.

GENERAL COMMENTS

Although Ox-eye Daisy is considered a persistent and invasive weed in many areas of North America, making it a serious problem for native plants, wildlife, and agriculture, in Nova Scotia it is not known to cause ecological problems. This low-growing plant has a long period of beautiful white blooms. On our roadsides it is commonly in bloom with Red Clover, Hawkweed, Vetch, and Birdsfoot-trefoil.

PEARLY EVERLASTING

Anaphalis margaritacea (L.) Benth. & Hook.

PEARLY EVERLASTING is an erect, branching plant that grows in colonies on roadside shoulders and back slopes. This native of Nova Scotia blooms from early August to late September, the flowers lasting into winter. The leaves are lance shaped and slightly rolled at the edges. This woolly plant is 30 to 80 cm tall, becoming more noticeable in the late summer and fall, when there are fewer plants in flower. It is common throughout the province.

Family: Asteraceae or Aster Family

HABITAT

Thrives in full sun.
Usually prefers dry or well-drained soils and gravel.
Can be found along gravelly shoulder sites on roadsides and hillsides.

GENERAL COMMENTS

This familiar wildflower adds a vibrant white colour to the landscape. On roadsides it often provides a beautiful display with the yellow of goldenrods, another gorgeous late-blooming native perennial.

RED CLOVER (*Trifolium pratense*), CREEPING WHITE CLOVER
(*Trifolium repens*), and ALSIKE CLOVER (*Trifolium
hybridum*) are the three most common perennial clover species
found in Nova Scotia, the third species being a hybrid between
the other two. Flower colour is purplish red for Red Clover,
white for White Clover, and light pink for Alsike Clover. All are
grown as forage crops, and all are introduced. Clovers are char-
acterized by leaves with three oval leaflet and by their clusters
of tiny, pea-shaped flowers.

Family: Fabaceae or Pea Family

HABITAT

Thrive in full sun.
Tolerant of different soils.
Usually grown as forage crops, but spreading freely
    to field, lawns, and roadsides.

GENERAL COMMENTS

As nitrogen-fixing plants, clovers are often seeded with grasses as forage crops and for soil cover to improve and maintain
soil fertility. They withstand mowing, or may be left alone.
Their long blooming period makes their flowers particularly
useful for bees.

*Red
Clover*

*White
Clover*

RAGGED ROBIN

RAGGED ROBIN is an introduced perennial species from Europe that grows 20 to 50 cm high. Its blue-green leaves are lance shaped, becoming more rounded further up the stem. It has the typical flat *Lychnis* inflorescence, but with just a few individual flowers instead of many. The flowers vary from purplish pink to white and have deeply cut petals.

Family: Caryophyllaceae or Pink Family

HABITAT

Prefers full sun.
Thrives in damp, neutral to alkaline soils.
Usually found growing in wet meadows, fields, and roadside ditches.

GENERAL COMMENTS

Ragged Robin is a garden escape that makes a beautiful showing when a large enough grouping of plants is established. In roadside ditches it persists and spreads slowly. Ragged Robin attracts butterflies, bumblebees, hoverflies, and other insects.

ROUGH CINQUEFOIL

ROUGH CINQUEFOIL is a branched, hairy annual or biennial, native to Nova Scotia and found throughout the province. Its leaves are divided into three leaflets (most cinquefoils have five) and are green on both sides. The erect, branched stems, which grow 30 to 50 cm high, bear small (7 to 10 mm wide) yellow flowers in July.

Family: Rosaceae or Rose Family

HABITAT

Thrives in full sun.

Prefers well-drained, acidic, sandy soils but is adaptable to other soil types.

Usually found in old fields, roadsides, and thickets.

GENERAL COMMENTS

The upright but low-growing habit, the ability to grow in disturbed soils, and the bright-yellow flowers make Rough Cinquefoil an appealing wildflower. It has been used as a medicinal herb.

ST. JOHN'S-WORT is a weedy perennial, introduced from Europe and now widely naturalized here. It is one of seven *Hypericum* species in Nova Scotia; the other six are native and grow in moist to wet soils. St. John's-wort grows 30 to 90 cm tall. Its showy flowers are bright yellow, with small black dots along the margins, and bloom from June to September.

Family: Clusiaceae or St. John's-wort Family

HABITAT

Prefers full sun.
Thrives in sand to gravel soils.
Usually found in pastures, meadows, roadsides,
    and waste places.

GENERAL COMMENTS

Each plant produces an abundance of seeds after flowering in the second year. St. John's-wort has been used as a medicinal herb, and in gardens for its bright yellow flowers. It is considered a noxious weed in many areas of North America and much effort has gone into finding biological control agents. When ingested by animals, a toxic substance photosensitizes the animal and causes irritation and loss of weight.

SULPHUR CINQUEFOIL

SULPHUR CINQUEFOIL is a non-native perennial introduced from Europe that grows 30 cm to 1 m in height. The leaves are palmately compound with five to seven narrow, hairy, toothed leaflets. The pale-yellow flowers have five notched petals, bloom in July, and are borne in a flat, terminal cluster. Sulphur Cinquefoil spreads from new shoots emerging from the edges of the root mass. It also spreads by seed and there is some evidence that it forms a persistent seed bank.

Family: Rosaceae or Rose Family

HABITAT

Tolerates sun and part shade.
Adapted to various soil types.
Adapted to a wide range of environmental conditions: grasslands, shrubby areas, logged areas, roadsides, waste areas and abandoned fields.

GENERAL COMMENTS

Sulphur Cinquefoil has attractive yellow flowers when in bloom and adds to our wildflower landscape. As a strong competitor occurring in early successional stages on roadsides and other disturbed places, however, it can form large monocultures and is not easily discouraged by mowing. It also has a high tannin content and is unpalatable to wildlife and livestock.

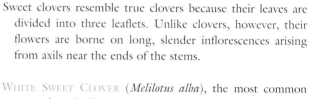

Sweet clovers resemble true clovers because their leaves are divided into three leaflets. Unlike clovers, however, their flowers are borne on long, slender inflorescences arising from axils near the ends of the stems.

WHITE SWEET CLOVER (*Melilotus alba*), the most common sweet clover in Nova Scotia, is a major problem on our roadsides because of its height (1–3 m) and dense growth habit. The plant has three leaflets with fine, sharp teeth and white flowers that bloom between June and October of its second year. This plant prefers a higher pH, thus is common in gypsum and limestone areas, on roadsides, and in towns, especially where soils have been disturbed. White Sweet Clover is scattered throughout Nova Scotia but is especially common from Annapolis to Pictou counties and in Halifax.

YELLOW SWEET CLOVER (*Melilotus officinalis*) is shorter and slightly more slender than the White Sweet Clover, has yellow flowers, and blooms a bit earlier. It is found from Annapolis to Lunenburg counties in the south, Cape Breton in the north, and is especially common in the Windsor/Maitland area, where gypsum is common.

Family: Fabaceae or Pea Family

White Sweet Clover

White Sweet Clover in flower

Thrive in sunny conditions.

Prefer soils with higher pH but are tolerant of
various soil conditions.

Found on disturbed sites, waste ground, and roadside
shoulders and backslopes.

*White Sweet
Clover, first-
year plant in
early July*

General Comments

Imported from Europe, sweet clovers are a source of nectar
for honey bees, have been used as medicinal plants, and are
grown as forage crops and soil improvers. Yellow and White
Sweet Clover make a beautiful showing when in full bloom,
particularly in grassy fields, but both species are invasive,
crowding out native vegetation in natural areas and interfer-
ing with sight lines along roadsides. As nitrogen fixers, they
quickly establish themselves on poor, infertile soil.

TALL WHITE ASTER

TALL WHITE ASTER is a white-flowering perennial with a smooth stem and lance-shaped leaves that have rough margins but are not toothed. It can reach heights of over a metre and flowers from July to October. The white flower heads are borne in a branched, flat-topped cluster 10 to 20 cm wide.

Family: Asteraceae or Aster Family

HABITAT

Prefers full sun.

Found in variable soil conditions in dry to moist areas.

Usually seen in roadside ditches and other moist
places such as swamps and marshes.

GENERAL COMMENTS

This native wildflower's white flower heads are quite showy along roadsides and moist waste places in late summer. It's one of the first asters to bloom, attracts butterflies, and would be a useful component of restoration seed mixes of native grasses and wildflowers for moist sites where a quick growth of vegetation is needed to stabilize the soil surface.

TANSY is a tall, aromatic perennial that grows in clumps 40 to 150 cm tall. Its leaves are fern-like and finely divided and have a strong odor. The yellow, button-like flower heads, 6 to 10 m across, bloom from July to August. Tansy was introduced from Europe and is now found throughout Nova Scotia along roadsides and in fields and orchards, especially in the Minas Basin area.

Family: Asteraceae or Aster Family

HABITAT

Thrives in sunny conditions.
Grows in variable soils.
Usually found along roadsides and in waste places.

GENERAL COMMENTS

Tansy has a long history in North America as a medicinal herb. Cultivation has assisted its spread throughout North America, including Nova Scotia. In some areas it is listed as a noxious weed and is thought to threaten ecological health by reducing wildlife habitat and species diversity. Because of its strong smell, Tansy is a natural insect repellent.

THREE-TOOTHED CINQUEFOIL

THREE-TOOTHED CINQUEFOIL is a dwarf native evergreen perennial that is found from Greenland to Alberta and as far south as Georgia. A pioneer plant on disturbed rocky or sandy sites, Three-tooth Cinquefoil spreads primarily through its root system, rather than by seeds. The stem is depressed and branching with glossy, leathery, compound leaves made up of three leaflets, each with three teeth at the end. The white, five-petaled flowers bloom from late May to August. Three-toothed Cinquefoil occurs in community with *Empetrum nigrum* on sandy, acidic soils. The leaves often turn red during the winter.

Family: Rosaceae or Rose Family

HABITAT

Full sun, to part shade.

Grows in sandy, rocky, or gravelly soils that are moist, acidic, and well-drained soils.

Bare and exposed locations, coastal, granite-rock outcrops.

GENERAL COMMENTS

Three-toothed Cinquefoil thrives in exposed rocky or sandy sites, forming large, attractive, dark-green patches; when in bloom it forms a carpet of white flowers. A colonizing plant in ideal conditions, it could be threatened by habitat destruction.

TOADFLAX OR BUTTER-AND-EGGS

TOADFLAX or BUTTER-AND-EGGS is an introduced perennial that spreads by creeping roots and winged seeds that are readily dispersed. The unbranched stems bear many long, narrow, grey-green leaves. The yellow, snapdragon-type flowers form in compact clusters on the end of the stems, have an orange tip on the lower petals and an elongated spur at the base, and bloom from July until August. It has a spreading growth habit and height of only 10 to 30 cm.

Family: Scrophulariaceae or Snapdragon Family

HABITAT

Prefers full sun.
Thrives in dry, gravelly or sandy soils.
Usually found along roadsides and in waste places.

GENERAL COMMENTS

Butter-and-eggs is a serious weed in agricultural systems and in gardens, but along roadside shoulders, patches of its pale yellow blooms form a cheerful display throughout the summer. An invasive plant, it aggressively displaces native vegetation in many habitats. It was brought to North America in the mid-1800s as an ornamental, and is used to make yellow dye and reportedly also for medicinal purposes.

TUFTED VETCH

TUFTED VETCH is the most common of the eight vetch species found in Nova Scotia. Vetches are vine-like annuals or perennials that form sprawling mats or engulf other species. Their leaves are alternate, pinnately compound, and end in a tendril. Tufted Vetch is a perennial with 5 to 11 pairs of leaflets per leaf, spreading rhizomes, and trailing stems up to 1 or 2 m long. The flowers are bluish-purple, arranged along one side of a long, stalked raceme (a distinguishing feature), and bloom in July and August. The seed pods turn brown at maturity.

Family: Fabaceae or Pea Family

HABITAT

Prefers sun to part shade.
Thrives in sand or gravel soils, but is tolerant of other types.
Usually found in waste places, roadsides, meadows,
  pastures, and as a weed in landscapes.

GENERAL COMMENTS

Tufted Vetch is a colourful plant with a long blooming period, and it mixes beautifully with other summer roadside flowers. It also attracts bees and butterflies and improves soil fertility through its nitrogen-fixing properties. However, Tufted Vetch can be invasive, its spreading roots making it difficult to control in gardens and agricultural systems.

WILD CARAWAY

WILD CARAWAY is a tall introduced species from Eurasia, and the only species of *Carum* in Nova Scotia. It is a smooth plant with divided, narrowly cut leaves resembling those of Wild Carrot. The hairless stems are hollow, and the numerous small white flowers are borne in umbels. Wild Caraway blooms earlier than Wild Carrot, in mid-June, and has maturing seed by the time Wild Carrot is in bloom.

Family: Apiaceae or Carrot Family

HABITAT

Thrives in full sun.
Prefers damp, fertile or infertile soils.
Usually found in damp fields, around houses,
   and on roadside shoulders and slopes.

GENERAL COMMENTS

Wild Caraway is an escaped garden plant that has been cultivated as a medicinal plant for a long time, mainly for its edible seeds. The white flowers are quite showy when massed along roadsides or other waste places.

WILD CARROT or QUEEN ANNE'S LACE

Daucus carota L.

An introduced species from Europe, WILD CARROT can be seen blooming along Nova Scotia highways from July to September. Its numerous creamy-white flowers are borne in an umbel with a flat top. The flowers form a lace-like pattern that often has a single, tiny, deep-purple floret in its centre. At maturity the flower cluster may resemble a bird's nest. The alternate, fern-like leaves are finely divided and subdivided. Wild Carrot is a biennial that spreads by seed. In its first year it forms a rosette of leaves. The flowering stalk, which appears in the second year, can reach 60 to 90 cm. One plant can produce up to 4000 seeds. The seeds have barbed prickles and consist of two halves that separate when mature.

Family: Apiaceae or Carrot Family

HABITAT
Prefers sun.
Thrives in dry, well-drained soils.
Usually found in pastures, meadows, and waste places.

GENERAL COMMENTS
The fragrant white flowers of Wild Carrot are a cheerful addition to Nova Scotia's roadside shoulders and back slope communities when it is blooming in August and on into the fall. This is the wild form of the cultivated carrot and although it invades disturbed ground, it is rarely of management concern.

WILD STRAWBERRY is a ground-hugging native plant with numerous runners that sometimes grows with Cinquefoil to form a dense ground cover. Its white flowers, with their five round petals, bloom in May and June. The leaves have three coarse-toothed leaflets, and spring from the base of the plant. On roadsides, it is found throughout the province on shoulders, where it often forms a dense ground cover, and on grassy back slopes.

Family: Rosaceae or Rose Family

HABITAT
Thrives in full sun.
Tolerant of different soils.
Grows in old fields, roadsides,
    waste places, and meadows.

GENERAL COMMENTS
Wild Strawberry forms a dense carpet dotted with clean white flowers, then bright red fruit. The plants arise from short rootstocks anchored in the soil by tough roots. Wild Strawberry is an ideal edible ground cover.

YARROW

YARROW is a common part of the summer scene all over Nova Scotia. A perennial, it reproduces by seeds and creeping rhizomes. The leaves are feather-like, greyish green, and covered with fine, woolly hairs. The lower leaves form dense patches in a rosette; the upper leaves are arranged alternately on the stem. Yarrow blooms from July through September, its tiny white flowers packed into dense, flat-topped or rounded clusters. The plant is aromatic, with an odour like sage.

Family: Asteraceae or Aster Family

HABITAT

Prefers full sun.

Thrives in acid soils, although it is found on roadside shoulders that are not acidic. It is drought resistant.

Usually grows in pastures and on roadsides, gravelly banks, and sandy shores.

GENERAL COMMENTS

Yarrow is desirable for its long blooming season, its cheerful white flower heads, and its low growth habit. Its strong, spreading, matted rootstocks may be of value for erosion control. Mowing does not seem to suppress the plant.

SHRUBS

BAYBERRY

BAYBERRY is a low-growing native shrub found on seashores and roadsides. It has an upright (to 2.5 m) spreading growth habit, a somewhat mounded shape, and is multi-stemmed, forming dense colonies of lush greenery that can be ever-green in warmer areas of the province. Its simple, dark-green, leathery leaves are arranged alternately along the stem and serrated towards the tips. The foliage is aromatic when crushed. The flowers are borne in small (1 cm) uni-sexual catkins. In the fall the leaves turn a bronze colour, exposing the waxy, pale-blue fruit, which persist on the stem after leaf fall.

Family: Myricaceae or Bayberry Family

HABITAT

Prefers full sun.

Thrives in sandy, dry soils of low fertility.

Found in many seashore and roadside locations and is tolerant of salt spray.

GENERAL COMMENTS

Bayberry is an actinorhizal plant with nitrogen-fixing root nodules that allow it to thrive in nutrient-poor soils and make it an important plant in native ecosystems. The scented waxy coating of its berries is used to make candles. Cuttings of the plant root readily.

BEARBERRY is a mat-forming native shrub that is frequently
associated with lichens and junipers on exposed granite rocks
and grows from the arctic south to New England. Its simple
leaves are a dark shiny green on top, alternate on the stem,
and remain on the plant over winter. Pinkish or white bell-
shaped flowers appear in early June and are followed by
small, red, berry-like fruit. The prostrate stems, 30 to 60 cm
long, root at the nodes and are covered with white hairs. The
roots can extend a metre or more into the soil. Bearberry can
be propagated by seed, which must first be scarified and
stored for a while in the cold.

Family: Ericaceae or Heath Family

HABITAT:

Full sun, intolerant of shade
Sandy or gravelly, well-drained, nutrient-poor, acidic soils
Coastal, granite rock outcrops

GENERAL COMMENTS

Bearberry is useful on slopes for erosion control. It is an
attractive ground cover in sunny, sandy areas and along rock
walls. The branches with their red fruit are useful for fall decorations. The fruits last through the winter, providing food for
birds and small mammals. The leaves have been used for tanning leather, and a dye has been made from it. North
American native peoples used it in smudges and ate the berries.

BLACKBERRY

COMMON BLACKBERRY is an erect, arching native shrub that can reach a height of over 2 m but can also be somewhat trailing. The shiny, toothed leaves are arranged in five leaflets. White flowers bloom in profusion in June and July, provide a good show on roadsides, and are followed by large, juicy, black fruit. Blackberry is the most common bramble found in Nova Scotia, and is well-armed with thorns.

Family: Rosaceae or Rose Family

HABITAT

Thrives in full sun.
Prefers sandy soil.
Commonly found along roadsides, and in
old fields and open woodlands.

GENERAL COMMENTS

Common Blackberry's bright, white, showy flowers and edible black fruit make this a desirable plant in clearings and alongside country properties. However, it readily spreads and its prickly stems may deter its use in some areas.

Aromia melanocarpa (Michx.) Ell.

BLACK CHOKEBERRY

BLACK CHOKEBERRY and RED CHOKEBERRY (*Aronia arbutifolia*), the only two species of *Aronia*, are widely distributed throughout North America. In Nova Scotia, Red Chokeberry is more likely to be found in southwestern areas; Black Chokeberry is more common along the Atlantic Coast. Both species bloom in late spring with clusters of small, white, five-petaled flowers. Its glossy green leaves are noticeable in community with Bayberry, Wild Rose and the wild flower *Potentilla tridentata* in the acidic sandy soils of coal mining areas of western Cape Breton. Red Chokeberry produces red berries in the fall; Black Chokeberry produces purplish-black berries.

Family: Rosaceae or Rose Family

HABITAT

Full sun to part shade.
Adapts to many soil types; can grow in acidic soils.
Found in peat bogs, swamps, and on cliffs.

GENERAL COMMENTS

Black Chokeberry is good for naturalizing in borders and mass plantings. It forms colonies through suckering, provides food and shelter for wildlife, and has a spectacular wine-red fall colour. It survives in both low-lying wet areas and drier, sandy or rocky locations. The fruit is unappetizing for birds and may be poisonous for us.

BLACK CROWBERRY

BLACK CROWBERRY is a dwarf native evergreen shrub with multiple branches and short, needle-like leaves. This spreading prostrate shrub has small white flowers appearing in July to September, followed by black fruit. Black Crowberry forms extensive carpets throughout Nova Scotia, particularly along the shoreline, but is nearly absent along the Northumberland Strait.

Family: Empetraceae or Crowberry Family

HABITAT

Prefers open light conditions.
Prefers sandy, acidic, low-fertility or rocky soils.
Commonly found in bogs and on granite barrens,
    sea cliffs, and rocky headlands.

GENERAL COMMENTS

Black Crowberry closely resembles Broom-crowberry, and they are difficult to distinguish from each other. Black Crowberry thrives in acidic, infertile habitats, where its roots help stabilize sandy soils, and it is an important part of the Nova Scotia flora. It provides cover for small rodents, while the berries provide food for birds and other wildlife.

Sambucus canadensis L.

BLACK-BERRIED ELDER

BLACK-BERRIED ELDER and RED-BERRIED ELDER (p. 72) are the only two species of elderberry in Nova Scotia. These multi-stemmed, native deciduous shrubs reach heights of 2 to 3 m. Flat-topped clusters of showy, creamy-white flowers bloom from mid- to late July, a little later than Red-berried Elder. The wedge-shaped, opposite leaves are pinnately compound, have 5 to 7 leaflets, and are lighter green beneath. Especially found in central Nova Scotia.

Family: Caprifoliaceae or Honeysuckle Family

HABITAT

Prefers full sun to part shade.
Usually found in damp, rich soils.
Grows in open woods, around old fields, and along streams.

GENERAL COMMENTS

Common or Black-berried Elder suckers readily and forms colonies. The edible blue-black fruits are attractive to birds and are commonly used to produce wine and jellies. Cuttings of dormant stems can be used in bioengineering projects.

BLACK HUCKLEBERRY

Gaylussacia baccata (Wang.) K. Koch

HUCKLEBERRY fruits were historically used as a substitute for blueberries. This shrub has oblong leaves with yellow spots on the underside, grows to 1 m tall, and commonly forms colonies. The reddish flowers appear in early June and are followed by smooth, black fruit. Black Huckleberry turns a brilliant scarlet in the fall. It is one of the most common shrubs found in rocky pastures, barrens, and mature bogs throughout the province. Bog Huckleberry (*G. dumosa*), a related species, is found in Yarmouth and along the Atlantic coast

Family: Ericaceae or Heath Family

HABITAT

Is adaptable to sun and shade conditions.
Prefers acidic soils in both wet and dry areas.
Found in rocky pastures, barrens, and mature bogs.

GENERAL COMMENTS

Black Huckleberry is a native shrub and should be enhanced and encouraged wherever possible. Its low-growing habit, bright fall colour, and adaptability to various growing conditions make this plant a desirable shrub.

BROOM-CROWBERRY is a wiry, highly branched shrub that forms dense evergreen mats only 15 to 20 cm high and has small, needle-like leaves. In early May, Broom-crowberry bears tufts of tiny purple flowers at the ends of its stems; the male and female flowers are on different plants. The fruit is a black berry.

Family: Empetraceae or Crowberry Family

HABITAT

Prefers open light conditions.
Grows in sandy acidic, low-fertility or rocky soils.
Is commonly found in bogs and acidic barrens, and on
    sea cliffs and headlands.

GENERAL COMMENTS

This native of Nova Scotia occurs abundantly on roadsides in Kings and Colchester counties, while on the rocky barrens of Halifax County it thrives with Black Crowberry, which it closely resembles. In general, though, Broom-crowberry has a disjunct distribution—its populations scattered from Newfoundland south to New Jersey—and is considered endangered in the south of its range. Especial care should thus be taken to protect it from habitat destruction.

BUSH HONEYSUCKLE

BUSH HONEYSUCKLE is a deciduous, low-growing, bushy native shrub that has a maximum height of 1 m and forms extensive patches on roadside shoulders and back slopes. The leaves are finely serrated, pointed at the tips, and medium to dark green with a purplish tinge. The flowers are yellow and resemble honeysuckle blooms. Bush Honeysuckle is found from Newfoundland to Saskatchewan and south to the mountains of North Carolina. It suckers readily.

Family: Caprifoliaceae or Honeysuckle Family

HABITAT

Prefers open, exposed areas with windy conditions.
Thrives in dry to moist, well-drained, infertile soils
    but also adapts to higher pH soils.
Can tolerate a variety of soils: gravel, sand, or loams.
Usually found along back slopes, roadsides, and in
    thickets and rocky pastures.

GENERAL COMMENTS

Bush Honeysuckle is an attractive, low-growing, sprawling, trouble-free native shrub that easily reproduces by seed and from rhizomes. If occasionally mowed, it regenerates from roots. It spreads, holds soil, and is tolerant of a wide range of soils and conditions.

CANADA HOLLY

CANADA HOLLY is a deciduous shrub, native to Nova Scotia and common throughout the province. It grows to about 2 m in an upright, spreading form, and establishes large clumps through suckering. The leaves have serrated margins, are wide above the middle, and can vary from green to dark green and dull to shiny, depending on the environmental conditions. The small, white, inconspicuous flowers appear in July. Since the plant is dioecious, there must be male plants around to ensure pollination.

Family: Aquifoliaceae or Holly Family

HABITAT

Prefers full sun to partial shade.
Tolerant of poorly drained soils and prefers acidic,
    moist to wet soils.
Found at the edges of woods and in damp
    places along streams and lakes.

GENERAL COMMENTS

Although its fall leaf colour is not very showy but the brilliant red fruits of female Canada Holly, or Winterberry, hold over into winter after the leaves are shed and bring the fall and winter landscape alive with colour. Canada Holly branches are a favourite Christmas decoration.

CRANBERRY

Vaccinium spp.

SMALL and LARGE CRANBERRY are two of the most common native species in Nova Scotia. These low, trailing evergreens are found in boggy, wet areas as well as on roadsides that have wet to moist, acidic soils. Both species bear red berries.

Family: Ericaceae or Heath Family

SMALL CRANBERRY (*Vaccinium macrocarpon*) has leaves less than 1 cm long, and berries that are 6 to 12 mm in diameter. The little white flowers are borne on a slender stem in late June.

LARGE CRANBERRY (*Vaccinium oxycoccus*) has larger leaves, longer than 1 cm, and its berries are 9 to 14 mm in diameter. Little, pale pink, cup-shaped flowers appear in June. This species is produced commercially in cranberry bogs.

Thrive in sun.

Prefer wet, damp, acidic, peat-rich soils.

Can be found in wet, boggy areas and swamps, and on
roadsides.

General Comments

The long trailing stems of these two species form a dense,
deep-green cover on moist or boggy acidic soils. They are
not very noticeable during the summer, when taller plants
dominate the vegetation, but in fall their red berries are available for eating. Being evergreen plants, they retain their
leaves, but they turn red in the fall to form a colourful carpet
that persists through the winter and spring. The plants are
shallow rooted and dislike disturbance.

HIGHBUSH-CRANBERRY is native to Nova Scotia, and though found from Annapolis and Cumberland counties to northern Cape Breton, generally along swamps and streams, it is more common eastward. This deciduous shrub has a dense, rounded crown and grows to a height of 4 m with an equal spread. The simple, dark-green leaves are three-lobed, 5 to 12 cm long, and opposite on the stem. Showy clusters of white flowers bloom in June and early July. Notably, the outer flowers of each cluster are sterile and larger than the rest. The bright-red fruit hang in clusters.

Family: Caprifoliaceae or Honeysuckle Family

HABITAT

Tolerates sun to partial shade.
Prefers well-drained, moist soils.
Usually found on the edges of fields,
meadows and swampy areas.

GENERAL COMMENTS

Highbush-cranberry can be planted and encouraged in areas with moist soil. The fall leaf colour can be yellowish red but often the leaves drop off while green. By winter the shrivelled fruits look like red raisins.

JUNIPER, COMMON

COMMON or GROUND JUNIPER is a creeping native evergreen shrub with sharp, flat, needle-like leaves that are 7 to 22 mm long and have a felt-like covering underneath and a white stripe on top. The foliage is grey green to blue green but turns brownish during winter. Common Juniper prefers sandy areas on roadsides, bogs, and old pastures throughout Nova Scotia, particularly in Cumberland and Annapolis Counties. The plants are 30 to 50 cm high and bear round, berry-like fruit that become bluish with maturity.

Family: Cupressaceae or Cypress Family

HABITAT

Prefers full-light conditions.
Adapts to different pHs and to poorly drained, infertile soils.
Usually found in sandy, rocky areas and on hillsides.
Tolerant of wind.

GENERAL COMMENTS

Common Juniper can be used in naturalistic plantings as a ground cover, especially in rocky, difficult, hard-to-mow areas. It is adaptable, thrives in full sun and windy conditions, and tolerates pollution and salt. It does not regenerate after being mowed. The cones are a favourite of birds in winter and are used to flavour gin.

JUNIPER, CREEPING

CREEPING JUNIPER is a prostrate native evergreen shrub with tiny, scale-like leaves. It grows in large mats 1 to 2 m in diameter and 30 to 50 cm tall. The foliage is blue green to green in the summer and turns a dull purple colour during the winter months. The bluish, berry-like cones are borne along the stems. Creeping Juniper is typically found on rocky headlands, cliffs, and bogs scattered along the Bay of Fundy. There are few populations along the Atlantic coast except in northern Cape Breton, where it is common.

Family: Cupressaceae or Cypress Family

HABITAT

Grows in full sun.

Adaptable to a range of pH and soils and has a tolerance for salt.

Usually found on gravelly slopes, cliffs, seaside locations, old pastures, and bogs.

GENERAL COMMENTS

This native juniper is less prickly than Common Juniper. It is tolerant of a wide range of conditions but does best in hot, sunny locations with dry, infertile soil where other shrubs may not survive. It is useful for erosion control.

LABRADOR TEA is a low-growing, acid-loving, native evergreen shrub. It is less than 1 m tall and its many branches are covered with dense, rusty-coloured hairs. The leathery leaves are alternate, narrowly oblong, and drooping. Their edges are tightly rolled under and there are dense, rust-coloured woolly hairs on the underside. Loose umbrella-like clusters of white flowers with five separate petals appear at the ends of the branches in mid- to late May.

Family: Ericaceae or Heath Family

HABITAT

Prefers partial shade but can tolerate sun conditions.
Tolerates acidic, sandy soil.
Can be found in bogs, swamps, and moist woods but also occasionally along roadsides.

GENERAL COMMENTS

Labrador Tea forms extensive carpets with species that thrive in similar nutrient-poor conditions. These dwarf shrub communities provide a far more effective soil cover than grasses and clovers in such places. The plant has a spicy fragrance and, as the name implies, it is used to make tea.

LAMBKILL

LAMBKILL or SHEEP LAUREL is a native evergreen shrub found throughout the province. Along roadsides, it is often part of the native flora retained during construction. It grows slowly to 1 m, has a spreading habit, and is often seen in large beds. The leaves are simple, arranged opposite or whorled on the stems, elliptical in shape, 2 to 5 cm long, and blue green in colour, with the lower surfaces powdery white. There is no fall colour. Lambkill is readily identified by its cup-shaped, rose-pink flowers, which appear in May to July after the new leaves and below them on the stem. The fruit has no ornamental value. As the name implies, this plant is poisonous.

Family: Ericaceae or Heath Family

HABITAT

Prefers partial to full sun.

Thrives in variable conditions—from dry to moist, and sandy to acid, organic soils.

Typically located in pastures and on barrens, roadsides and open ground.

The low, spreading habit and beautiful, bell-shaped, rose-pink flowers make this native plant a desirable shrub for acid, organic soils. During construction activities, beds of this plant should be retained whenever possible. It is, however, a problem "weed" in blueberry fields since it readily regenerates after burning. An evergreen shrub, it returns little leaf litter to the soil, but nevertheless builds up soil humus through root die-off. It responds to transplanting by sprouting from root suckers. It has been used in the reclamation of peat mines.

LEATHERLEAF

Chamaedaphne calyculata (L.) Moench

The only species in its genus, LEATHERLEAF is found throughout Canada and south into New England, and has a distinctive rusty appearance. The oval leaves often fold above the stem, appearing to arise on one side of the stem, and are smaller toward the top. White, vase-shaped flowers appear near the ends of branches from mid-May to mid-June, looking a little like lily of the valley. Leatherleaf is one of the most common shrubs of acidic bogs in Nova Scotia. It is low-growing (1 m), native, and evergreen.

Family: Ericaceae or Heath Family

HABITAT

Prefers shade to part sun but can withstand sunny areas.
Thrives in acid, peaty soils.
Usually found along wet ditches, in bogs and at lake margins.

GENERAL COMMENTS

Leatherleaf is a desirable, moisture-loving plant suitable for bog and wetland areas. It is acid-tolerant and usually occurs where the pH is less than 5. Where it is the dominant shrub on a site, conditions are clearly acidic. Forms dense thickets.

MEADOWSWEET is one of our two native species of *Spiraea*. It is a small (to 70 cm), wiry, branched shrub with simple, toothed leaves. The white flowers are about 5 mm wide, have round petals, and are arranged on a loose, pyramid-shaped panicle. The seed head is quite distinctive in winter. Common on roadsides throughout Nova Scotia.

Family: Rosaceae or Rose Family

HABITAT

Grows well in full sun.
Tolerant of soils and prefers moist soils.
Found in low-lying areas, ditches, and swamps.

GENERAL COMMENTS

This small shrub is prolific in roadside ditches and is adapted to a range of soils, although it likes moist areas. It roots easily from cuttings, spreads quickly, and is useful for bioengineering projects on moist slopes and along the banks of watercourses. The flowers have value for bees and butterflies, and the twigs may be browsed by deer and rabbits.

RED-BERRIED ELDER

RED-BERRIED ELDER is a multi-stemmed deciduous native shrub that grows 1.5 to 3 m tall and is common throughout the province except in northern Cape Breton. It has dark-green, pinnately compound leaves with serrated margins, and bears creamy-white flowers in early July. The bright-red berries are poisonous, but make a spectacular showing on our roadsides.

Red-berried Elder is adapted to drier areas, has poisonous berries, and its inflorescence is pyramid shaped. Black-berried Elder, on the other hand, prefers moister soils, has edible berries, and has a flat-topped inflorescence.

Family: Caprifoliaceae or Honeysuckle Family

HABITAT

Prefers sun or partial shade.
Prefers dry to damp soils and will tolerate a range of pH.
Usually found in meadows and wet places,
    on rocky hillsides, and along streams.

The pyramidical clusters of white flowers and bright red berries make this a showy plant of roadsides and waste areas. It establishes slowly, but grows well on moist sites and occasionally on seeps. It is easy to transplant, can be propagated by cuttings and division, spreads readily, and is useful in the naturalistic landscape. Dormant cuttings can be used in bio-engineering to help stabilize slopes and the plant can be useful in controlling erosion on moist sites. Recommended for planting on disturbed riparian areas.

RED OSIER DOGWOOD

RED OSIER DOGWOOD is a native deciduous shrub found on roadsides and ditches throughout most of Nova Scotia. This low, spreading shrub reaches a height of about 1 m and bears flat clusters of white flowers in June that later turn to white berries. The lance-shaped, opposite leaves turn a rich red in the fall. The red twigs are attractive in the winter, particularly with a backdrop of snow.

Family: Cornaceae or Dogwood Family

HABITAT

Grows best in full sun.
Prefers moist soil, but will adapt to drier sites.
Tolerates flooding, and typically grows in roadside ditches, on streambanks, and in wetter areas of fields.
Spreads by root suckers and by layering.

The bright red stems of a large stand of Red Osier Dogwood are conspicuous and showy in winter against a background of snow, and on into spring. It has great cold tolerance and is very adaptable to different soils, as long as moisture is adequate. It is easily propagated by separating suckers at the base of the plant and replanting them. Dormant cuttings can be used in bioengineering projects.

RED RASPBERRY

RED RASPBERRY has a biennial stem and perennial rootstock and is 1 to 2 m tall. An introduced species, it is usually one of the first plants to establish after land is disturbed. Its leaves are divided into 3 to 5 leaflets that are white underneath, and there are prickles on the erect branches or canes. Small clusters of inconspicuous white flowers bloom in July. Fruit is produced on the second year canes, and is ripe in August. Red Raspberry seeds germinate after they are digested and dispersed by birds and can remain viable in the soil for many years. Germination will occur once the soil conditions are favorable. Red Raspberry is common throughout the province.

Family: Rosaceae or Rose Family

HABITAT

Prefers full sun.

Grows best in sandy, rocky soil.

Usually found on roadsides, deforested land, old fields, and rocky areas.

GENERAL COMMENTS

Red Raspberry is suitable for rough areas. On disturbed sites, it minimizes nutrient losses. It helps provide erosion control and provides cover for birds and small mammals. The red berries are tasty for humans and animals alike. Solid patches suppress tree invasion.

RHODORA

RHODORA is a low-growing native species that grows up to 1 m tall. In May, its beautiful magenta blooms dot roadsides where conditions favour its presence (acidic, wet soils). Rhodora is found from Newfoundland to Quebec, south to New Jersey and Pennsylvania. The two-lipped flowers appear before the leaves, which are smooth and oval. Rhodora can be propagated by seeds or cuttings but does not transplant well.

Family: Ericaceae or Heath Family

HABITAT

Grows best in sunny areas.

Prefers coarse to medium-textured soils.

Found in acidic bogs, swamps, and abandoned wet pastures, and on rocky barrens and roadsides.

GENERAL COMMENTS

One of our more beautiful indigenous spring-flowering shrubs on moist, infertile, acidic soils. The magenta flowers blend well with nearby plants, many of which are also in the Heath Family. It has low browsing interest for wildlife, and there is some evidence that it may produce toxic substances that inhibit the growth of trees.

SPECKLED and DOWNY ALDER

Alnus spp.

DOWNY ALDER (*Alnus viridis*) and SPECKLED ALDER (*A. incana*) are the two most common species of alder in Nova Scotia. Downy Alder is distinguished from Speckled Alder by its soft, downy twigs. These large native shrubs or small trees have coarse, oval leaves with serrated margins and bear both male and female catkins. The pendulous male catkins appear in the fall and release their pollen in early spring. The smaller female catkins develop into woody cones when mature.

Family: Betulaceae or Birch Family

HABITAT

Thrive in sun and shade.
Prefer poorly drained soils.
Streams, moist areas, and abandoned fields.

GENERAL COMMENTS

Alders are often considered to be undesirable because of their height and their tendency to invade areas with poorly drained soils, forming dense stands. However, Alder's ability to fix atmospheric nitrogen make it an important part of nutrient cycling in native ecosystems. Alders also provide habitat for wildlife and fish by shading pools. They are important as colonizers in returning disturbed lands to forest.

STAGHORN SUMAC

STAGHORN SUMAC is a large shrub or small tree, 4 to 6 m tall, that is found throughout Nova Scotia but is more abundant in southwestern counties. Its forked branches have a velvety covering and resemble deer antlers, hence the name. The pinnately compound leaves have 5 to 15 leaflets and are alternate on the stems. The tiny, yellowish-green flowers are borne in large, hairy panicles, with the male flower head larger than the female and usually on a separate plant. In fall the leaves turn from yellow to orange to red; the dense clusters of fuzzy, deep-red berries at the top of the tree persist throughout winter.

Family: Anacardiaceae or Cashew Family

HABITAT

Prefers full sun but tolerates shade.

Adaptable to different soils.

Found on roadsides, hillsides, and beside woods.

GENERAL COMMENTS

Staghorn Sumac has a fast rate of growth and is able to colonize large areas by suckers. It is particularly known for its vivid fall foliage, as well as its usefulness in erosion control. It grows well on rocky hillsides or dry banks with limestone-based soils. It can be propagated by seed or rooted cuttings.

STEEPLEBUSH

STEEPLEBUSH is a mostly unbranched low shrub that grows to 1 m tall. The underside of its serrated, oval leaves is densely covered in rusty hairs; the stems are also brown. In August, dense clusters of tiny, purple-rose flowers bloom on a slender, steeple-shaped panicle at the top of the plant. Steeplebush is common in central Nova Scotia and scattered throughout the rest of the province.

Family: Rosaceae or Rose Family

HABITAT

Grows well in full sun.
Prefers poorly drained, acid soils.
Found in low-lying areas, ditches, and swamps.

GENERAL COMMENTS

Steeplebush prefers a wetter habitat than our other *Spiraea*, Meadowsweet, which is much more commonly found. The fruit is persistent through the winter, providing food for birds. The leaves and bark have been used medicinally. It can be planted or used in seed mixtures for wet meadows or alongside watercourses. In moist areas with full sun it can be found associated with other acid-tolerant shrubs, including Black Chokeberry, Leatherleaf, Red Osier Dogwood, and blueberry.

SWEETFERN is one of the most common low-growing shrubs on Nova Scotian roadsides. It is a spreading, colonizing, deciduous shrub less than 1 m tall. The alternate, dark-green leaves are long and slender, with coarse, tooth-like lobes. The foliage is aromatic, especially when crushed. The flowers are small catkins, the fruit a cluster of nutlets. Each plant bears both male (olive-green) and female (dark-red) catkins. It is particularly abundant on the sandy soils of Kings and Cumberland counties and on granite soils elsewhere.

Family: Myricaceae or Bayberry Family

HABITAT

Prefers sun to partial shade.
Thrives in well-drained, sandy, acidic soils with low fertility.
    Does not compete well on more fertile sites.
Found on roadsides, hillsides, and sandy areas.

GENERAL COMMENTS

Sweetfern fixes nitrogen in a symbiotic association with *Frankia*, an actinomycete, and its cluster roots assist in phosphorus uptake. It is a pioneer colonizer of disturbed sites and is suitable for use in reclamation and in the stabilization of sandy slopes. Though difficult to transplant from the wild, Sweetfern can be propagated from root cuttings. Once established in the right soil, it readily forms large clumps.

SWEET GALE

SWEET GALE is an aromatic deciduous shrub native to Nova Scotia. Growing to a metre or so in height, it forms dense clumps around the edges of lakes, bogs, and swamps. Its blue-green leaves are lance shaped and toothed towards their ends, its stems dark brown and speckled with yellow. Sweet Gale's tiny flowers are borne in small catkins, with male and female catkins on different plants. Blooming occurs in April to early June. The nutlets smell like sage.

Family: Myricaceae or Bayberry Family

HABITAT

Prefers sun to partial shade.

Fine to medium-textured soils, pH 5 to 8; not very salt tolerant.

Usually found in bogs and swamps, and at the edges of ponds, lakes, and streams.

GENERAL COMMENTS

Sweet Gale, like Bayberry and Sweetfern, fixes atmospheric nitrogen in root nodules through a symbiotic association with a species of the actinomycete genus *Frankia*. It thrives on infertile, acidic, wet soils, and though it has some tolerance to drought, it cannot tolerate liming. With other plants in wetland communities, it provides important habitat for birds and other wildlife.

VIRGINIA CREEPER

VIRGINIA CREEPER or WOODBINE is a deciduous native vine that climbs buildings and trees with the aid of tendrils equipped with oval adhesive disks at their tips. The leaves are compound, have five leaflets, and are alternate on the stem. The flowers, which appear in late June to early July, are greenish and not showy; the fruits are black. The plant reproduces vegetatively by sprouting from horizontal, above-ground stems, and sexually through seeds that are dispersed by animals eating the fruit. The leaves turn a brilliant red in fall.

Family: Vitaceae or Grape Family

HABITAT
Full to partial sun.
Soil moist to dry, neutral to acid.
Moist woods, thickets, hillsides, rocky banks, roadsides, and cultivated areas.

GENERAL COMMENTS
Virginia Creeper is commonly cultivated as a cover on buildings, walls, porch screens, fences, and rock piles. It provides a luscious green during summer and a brilliant scarlet red in fall. The fruits provide fall and winter food for birds and small mammals, such as mice and squirrels, and the foliage is sometimes browsed by deer. The dense vine also affords cover for small wildlife.

WILD BLUEBERRY

WILD BLUEBERRY or LOWBUSH BLUEBERRY is the species harvested by commercial blueberry growers throughout Maine, New Brunswick, Nova Scotia and regions in Quebec. The small, white, bell-shaped flowers bloom at the ends of the branches in late May, and the fruit is ripe by mid- to late August. Wild Blueberry and Velvet-leaf Blueberry (*Vaccinium myrtilloides*) are the two most common blueberries in the province. Velvet-leaf Blueberry prefers part shade and is easily distinguished by its hairy stems and velvet, wavy leaves.

Family: Ericaceae or Heath Family

HABITAT

Prefers full sun.

Grows in sandy, acidic soils.

Found along roadsides, cliff areas, and rocky, sandy ground.

GENERAL COMMENTS

Wild Blueberry is a low-growing plant that spreads slowly by rhizomes. In the landscape it can be used in masses as groundcover. If burned or mowed every few years, it will spring back from the underground rhizomes, bursting with energy. The attractive flowers, the ecological value of the fruit to wildlife, and the fiery, crimson red autumn foliage make this a valuable native plant in the landscape.

WILD RAISIN or WITHEROD is a deciduous native shrub found
throughout Nova Scotia. It is dense and multi-stemmed,
growing to 2 m in both height and spread. The simple, elliptical leaves are opposite on the stem, and in June showy,
creamy-white flowers are borne in flat-topped clusters. The
berres ripen with a series of colour changes: from green to
white, then pink, and finally blue to bluish black.

Family: Caprifoliaceae or Honeysuckle Family

HABITAT

Likes full sun to part shade.
Prefers dry or moist, somewhat acidic soils. Usually found
along streams, lakes, edges of woods and pastures.

GENERAL COMMENTS

In masses, or as a low screen or specimen, Wild Raisin or
Witherod is a beautiful shrub with lustrous green foliage and
lovely white flowers. The attractive berries make a beautiful
showing with the red to reddish purple fall foliage.

WILD ROSE

WILD ROSE is the most common native rose in Nova Scotia and is found all over the Province. This coarse, prickly shrub can reach heights of 2 m, although it is often shorter. One or more pink flowers (5 to 7 cm wide) are borne on old wood in July. The leaves have 5 to 7 leaflets and turn a bright crimson in the fall; the red fruit persist into winter. *Rosa carolina*, which is also known as Wild Rose, has straighter thorns, is more slender, less common, and is found on drier sites.

Family: Rosaceae or Rose Family

HABITAT

Thrives in sun and partial shade.
Tolerates different soil types and is also salt tolerant.
Usually found along roadsides, old pastures, and
    coastal sites.

GENERAL COMMENTS

Wild Rose is a common shrub that spreads by suckering freely from underground stems and from roots. It forms dense, prickly thickets and can be used in hedgerows, providing cover for birds and small mammals. The leaves turn a scarlet colour in the fall and the bright-red fruit, or hips, make a nice contrast against snow, after the leaves have fallen. The fruit is eaten by many bird species, and can be used in jellies and as a tea.

GRASSES &
GRASS-LIKE
PLANTS

BENT-GRASSES

Nova Scotia has six species of BENT-GRASSES. Four of them were introduced as forage and turf grasses; the other two are native. Bent-grasses are tough, persistently perennial, fine-textured grasses. They grow to about 60 cm and spread by seeds and rhizomes. Two of the non-native species, RED TOP and BROWN TOP, are often part of reclamation seed mixes.

RED TOP (*Agrostis gigantea*) is sometimes seeded on Nova Scotia roadsides as part of a seed mix, and its reddish colour is a familiar sight during flowering.

BROWN TOP or COLONIAL BENT GRASS (*A. capillaris*) is also used for erosion control and remediation of contaminated lands.

NATIVE SPECIES OF BENT-GRASS
The two native species are *A. hyemalis* (Tickle-grass or Witch-grass) and *A. perennans.* Both are found in dry or moist soil in fields and woods, and on roadsides.

Family: Poaceae or Grass Family

Prefer full sun to part shade.
Tolerant of different soil types; moderately
    drought resistant and salt tolerant.
Found in pastures, meadows, fields, and roadsides.

GENERAL COMMENTS

Red Top and Brown Top both spread rapidly by seed and underground rhizomes. Red Top grows well on acidic and clayey sites. It is adapted to nutrient-poor, wet, poorly drained conditions and is used for pasture and hay in those areas. Red Top also does well in riparian areas and can be used to improve streambank stability.

BLUEGRASSES

*Kentucky
Bluegrass*

BLUEGRASSES found in Nova Scotia include four native species and five introduced lawn and forage species. Two of the native species, *Poa glauca* and *P. alsodes*, are considered rare.

Family: Poaceae or Grass Family

KENTUCKY BLUEGRASS (*Poa pratensis*) is adapted for growth in cool, humid climates and is widely distributed across North America. It is a dark-green leafy perennial grass whose creeping rootstocks form a dense sod.

HABITAT

Prefers part sun to shade conditions.

Grows in high-fertility soils with moderate amounts of moisture.

Common in pastures and meadows, and on roadsides and lawns.

GENERAL COMMENTS

Although Kentucky Bluegrass is part of the Nova Scotia Highway Seed Mix, it has limited value in rehabilitation work because it is slow to establish cover, is not drought-tolerant, and has high soil-fertility requirements. When planted in seed mixtures, it often takes two or three years to become established. Once established however, it is persistent and forms a dense sod that promotes soil stability. Because of its shallow root system, Kentucky Bluegrass is generally not as good a soil stabilizer as the native grasses it replaces. In riparian settings, it is ineffective in stabilizing streambanks. Kentucky Bluegrass is intolerant of prolonged flooding, high water tables, or poor drainage. The leaves and seeds are eaten by numerous species of small mammals and songbirds and it provides habitat for numerous species of small mammals.

CANADA BLUEGRASS (*Poa compressa*) is a non-native, bluish-green, flat-stemmed perennial with a long-running rootstock that forms an open sod. The panicles are narrow and usually 4 to 10 cm long with short, spreading branches. Canada Bluegrass flowers throughout the summer.

HABITAT

Prefers sunny conditions.

Grows in dry, sterile soils.

Usually found in meadows, pastures, dry roadside
banks and gravel areas, as well as worn-out fields.

GENERAL COMMENTS

Canada Bluegrass is an early colonizer of disturbed soils and is used in reclamation mixtures with legumes for cover and erosion control. It may be slow to establish but forms a loose open sod and provides good long-term cover on low-fertility soils with poor drainage.

BULRUSHES

BULRUSHES are a large group within the Sedge Family (Cyperaceae). These native perennial plants are easily distinguished from grasses and rushes by their solid stems and lack of stem nodes. The stems can be sharp to softly triangular, and the leaves can vary from obvious leaf blades to reduced sheaths. Inflorescences are always borne at the stem tips and can be in tight clusters or open and spreading. Bulrushes spread by seeds that can remain viable for many years before germination, and also by rhizomes.

There are many species of *Scirpus* in Nova Scotia, but *Scirpus cyperinus* is the most common, being found in wet meadows and swamps throughout the province. It usually grows to 2 m and is somewhat widely spaced in habit. The stems are topped by large, drooping, shaggy-brown inflorescences several centimetres long. Many brown, woolly bristles surround the nutlets, giving the cluster of spikelets a fuzzy appearance.

Other species common to Nova Scotia are *Scirpus americanus, Scirpus validus* and *Scirpus maritimus.*

Family: Cyperaceae or Sedge Family

Habitat

Tolerant of sun to part shade.

Soil type variable but generally prefers moist,
sandy, or peat soils.

Habitat can vary from salt water to fresh water,
depending on the species: bogs, alder thickets, swamps,
shallow marshes, sedge meadows, and roadside ditches.

General Comments

Bulrushes are important components of native
wetland ecosystems. Along the edge of ponds and
lakes, and in ditches, they help control erosion and trap
sediment. Bulrushes can be used in constructed wetlands with cat-tails and other wetland plants that,
together with the sediments and decaying plant matter
they trap, provide a habitat for microbes, allowing
them to remove nitrates and other pollutants from
wastewater. Bulrushes provide cover and habitat for
waterfowl and other wildlife, and their seeds are eaten
by many birds.

CAT-TAILS

CAT-TAILS are familiar native wetland plants reaching heights of 1 to 2 m. The velvety-brown, spike-shaped terminal flower head is a distinctive feature of the plant and the leaves are long and linear. Seeds are released in the fall and can remain viable in the seed bank for up to 100 years. Cat-tails also spread by rhizomes to form thick colonies. Nova Scotia is graced by two species: Broad-leaved Cat-tail (*Typha latifolia*) and Narrow-leaved Cat-tail (*T. angustifolia*).

Family: Typhaceae or Cat-tail Family

HABITAT

Prefer sun to part shade.

Tolerant of reduced soil conditions and moderate salinity.

Thrive in such wetland areas as bogs, freshwater marshes, wet ditches, and the edges of lakes and streams.

GENERAL COMMENTS

These common wetland plants provide excellent habitat, food, and breeding sites for birds and other animals. Cat-tails are sometimes referred to as the "supermarket of the swamp." Their young shoots, roots, and leaves are edible; they were used historically for herbal medicines; and they provide material for mats and thatching. Cat-tails are used in wetland restoration and for tertiary wastewater treatment.

Phragmites australis (Cav.) Trin.

With an average height of 2 m, COMMON REED is the tallest
native wetland perennial in Nova Scotia. You'll see it scattered throughout the province. Its purplish-brown, plume-
like inflorescence is 20 to 30 cm long and appears from late
July to September, but rarely sets seed. The stiff, hollow
stems support smooth, broad leaves.

Family: Poaceae or Grass Family

Habitat

Prefers sunny conditions.
Grows best in clay soils and tolerates moderate salinity and a
range of pH. Particularly prevalent in disturbed soils.
Usually found in wet areas such as swamps, marshes,
lakes, ditches, and at the edges of streams.

General Comments

Common Reed spreads by an extensive system of rhizomes
that allow the plant to form colonies and help to stabilize wet,
brackish soils. In some regions of North America, however,
the colonizing root system chokes out other native wetland
vegetation. Common Reed is frequently used in the
Mediterranean region and elsewhere in building dwellings,
lattices and fences, and for weaving mats. Acadians once
thatched their roofs with Common Reed; a replica roof can be
viewed at the Annapolis Historic Gardens.

CORD GRASSES

Of the three species of CORD GRASS native to Nova Scotia, two are restricted to saline habitats: SALT-MEADOW GRASS (*Spartina patens*) and CORD GRASS (*S. alterniflora*). The only freshwater species is FRESHWATER CORD GRASS (*S. pectinata*). All three are perennial and spread by rhizomes that form a dense, tough mat beneath the ground and prevent the soil from eroding away. Cord grasses reproduce both sexually by seeds and asexually by rhizomes.

FRESHWATER CORD GRASS is our tallest cord grass, reaching heights of 1 to 2 m. The leaves are smooth and shiny on the surface, taper off to a sharp point, and have sharp, tiny teeth on their margins, giving them an abrasive feel. The flowers are arranged in tight rows on one side of the flowering branches, like the teeth of a comb. A closely related European species has assumed great importance as a soil binder along the coastal areas of the Netherlands, northern France and southern England.

Family: Poaceae or Grass Family

S. pectinata:

Prefers sunny areas.

Occurs on most soil textures—from fine clays to silt
    loams—and is somewhat tolerant of alkaline conditions.

Tolerant of high water tables but intolerant
    of prolonged flooding.

Thrives in damp open areas, roadsides, marshy meadows,
    and along streams, dams, and ditches.

S. patens and *S. alterniflora*: salt marshes and tidal flats.

General Comments

Frequently the dominant plant in the salt marsh ecosystem,
Cord Grass plays a key role in the transition from sea life to
terrestrial communities. It provides cover and food for
wildlife and invertebrate species, and its dense, tough mat of
roots helps to stabilize and protect shorelines while trapping
sediment, detritus, and nutrients from terrestrial runoff.

The gathering and use of salt hay was a traditional industry
along Atlantic coasts, since it could be harvested annually
without cultivation it and had a wide range of uses: as insula-
tion, to cover bare soils during construction, as thatching
material, and as forage. Cord grasses are still sometimes used
for forage or cut for hay on coastal Nova Scotia farms.

FESCUES

FESCUES are found throughout Canada. They have a long history as introduced and native perennial species.

Family: Poaceae or Grass Family

Creeping Fescue

CREEPING RED FESCUE (*Festuca rubra* ssp. *arenaria*) is a narrow-leaved perennial grass with short-running rootstocks that produce new shoots and stems, giving the plant a tufted appearance. The dark-green leaves are folded in the bud-shoot but become flat when developed. Creeping Red Fescue is used for erosion control along roads and highways, cuts, fills, and other disturbed areas, and for stream-bank stabilization. It is part of the Nova Scotia Highway Seed Mix.

Festuca rubra can be distinguished from *F. ovina* by its dark-green colour, its habit of spreading, and its even or somewhat tufted turf. It also differs from *F. ovina* in having open leaves, although they may close in dry conditions. It requires more moisture and better soils than *F. ovina*.

HABITAT

Tolerant of shade.
Prefers gravel, calcareous, and sandy soils.
Usually found along roads and highways, and
     in disturbed areas.

MEADOW FESCUE (*Festuca pratensis*) is often seeded as part of reclamation seed mixes. Adapted to cool climates, this tufted, deep-rooted perennial grass grows to 80 cm. The leaves are long and slender, bright green and succulent.

HABITAT

Tolerant of some shade.
Prefers rich soils.
Usually found along roads, on riverbanks, in pastures and waste places.

SHEEP'S FESCUE (*Festuca ovina*) is a fibrous-rooted, densely tufted, narrow-leaved perennial that grows on poor, dry soils. The plants are yellowish green or bluish grey green, 20 to 50 cm high. The leaves are rolled in the bud and remain rolled even when developed. Horizontal rooting stems are absent.

HABITAT

Prefers exposed, sunny areas.
Tolerant of poor, dry, infertile soils with low pHs.
Generally found on roadsides and in pastures and lawns.

GENERAL COMMENTS

Fescues are used in seed mixtures for forage, lawns and land reclamation. Horticultural varieties have been developed for ornamental landscape use. Sheep's Fescue grows in acidic soils and is tolerant of shade.

Meadow Fescue

RUSHES are normally wetland plants, have hollow or pithy stems, and are common in roadside ditches and other moist or wet areas. There are about 200 species worldwide; more than 20 of them live in Nova Scotia., all of them native. Six species are listed as rare and one, New Jersey Rush, is listed as vulnerable by the Committee on the Status of Endangered Wildlife in Canada.

Family: Juncaceae or Rush Family

SPECIES YOU ARE LIKELY TO SEE:

RUSH (*J. pylaei*). Vigorous clumps over 1 m tall. Flowers are near top of plant, to one side of stem.

TOAD RUSH (*J. bufonius*). Low, 10–15 cm, much-branched annual. Single or paired flowers borne along the branches.

RUSH (*J. marginatus*). Slender, 20–40 cm tall, compressed stems, flower inflorescence is 2 to 4 cm long.

BLACK GRASS (*J. gerardii*). 30 cm tall, 1–4 leaves below the middle of the stem. Salt marshes, in overflow from cultivated fields.

RUSH (*J. tenuis*). 20–40 cm tall, flower inflorescence with branches, each with flowers along one side. Papery projection of leaf sheath. Common throughout Nova Scotia.

RUSH (*J. brevicaudatus*). Small, slender, 40–50 cm tall, dense clumps. Common throughout Nova Scotia.

SOFT RUSH (*Juncus effusus*). See p. 104 for a description.

Prefer sun to part shade.

Soils depend on the species, ranging from compacted to sandy, muddy, clay, or even peat.

Depending on the species, rushes are found in swamps, thickets, lakes, low meadows, roadside ditches, fields, salt marshes, on roadsides and at the edges of ponds.

GENERAL COMMENTS

Rushes are found in moist, marshy sites along with species of sedges, grasses, and wildflowers that like these poorly drained areas. These wetland plants provide food for waterfowl, birds, and mammals, as well as cover and shelter. Rushes reduce soil erosion and improve water quality by trapping sediment and pollutants. They can be used with other riparian plants in wet areas and in "constructed wetlands" for stormwater control, thus providing wildlife habitat and removing stormwater pollutants at the same time.

SEDGES

SEDGES are herbaceous, grass-like plants that grow in clumps and have a fibrous root system. Their sharp-edged leaves are arranged in three ranks along the stem; in grasses, the leaves are slender and are usually in two rows. The stems are solid and commonly triangular in cross-section, with leaves arising from the nodes. The flowers are usually clustered in spikelets, and mature fruit are usually necessary for identification.

Worldwide, there are about 1500 members of the genus *Carex*, with the greatest diversity occurring in north-temperate and arctic zones. *Roland's Flora of Nova Scotia* lists 106 Nova Scotian species.

Common sedge species found throughout Nova Scotia include *Carex stipata*, *Carex nigra*, *Carex pseudocyperus*, *Carex scoparia*, and *Carex aurea*.

Family: Cyperaceae or Sedge Family

Tolerant of sun to part shade.
Common in wet areas and poorly drained soils.
Usually found alongside streams and in bogs and wet ditches.

GENERAL COMMENTS

Many Nova Scotian habitats support sedges. Along lakeshores and in brackish marshes, sedges form an important part of the emergent herbaceous vegetation, and thriving in soils that are saturated to inundated by standing water throughout most of the growing season. Several species form dense stands; others are part of diverse communities. As part of these wetland communities, sedges are heavily utilized by wildlife and birds for shelter and food.

SOFT RUSH

SOFT RUSH is a native wetland plant with a deep, fibrous root system. This spreading, clump-forming perennial emerges from a branching rootstock and grows to about 1 m in height. It has no leaves, and the portion of the stem above the flowers is much shorter than that below. Soft Rush can be propagated from seed or vegetative divisions; stem divisions (bare root or containerized) are reliable for planting out before mid-June.

Family: Juncaceae or Rush Family

HABITAT

Thrives in direct sun.
Prefers finely textured soils with pHs from 4.0 to 6.0.
Found in fresh to brackish marshes, swamps, ditches
    and seasonally moist wetlands and meadows.

GENERAL COMMENTS

The deep fibrous root system of Soft Rush makes it an excellent plant for filtering sediments, stabilizing streambanks, and for erosion control in wet soils. It is a good candidate for replanting in wetland conditions during construction activities. Soft Rush is used for food and cover by waterfowl, song birds, and small mammals, and by humans for floor mats and chair seats. Its tolerance to low pH and metals allows it to survive polluted conditions.

Phleum pratense L.

TIMOTHY is a major cool-season perennial bunchgrass imported from Europe by early immigrants and one of the most
commonly planted forage grasses in Nova Scotia. It is also a
component of the Nova Scotia Highway Seed Mix and the
Prince Edward Island Highway Seed Mix.

Timothy has shallow, fibrous roots extending to more than
1 m. Its crown (where stem and roots meet) consists of a
group of bulb-like or swollen sections that produce a mass of
basal leaves and usually one leafy stem of 50 to 100 cm,
which ends in a seed head. All leaves are soft, light green and
5 to 15 cm long.

Family: Poaceae or Grass Family

HABITAT
Prefers full sun.
Adapted to somewhat poorly drained soils but not
    to soils subject to drought.
Usually found in forage fields, waste places, and roadsides.

Timothy is a valuable forage grass in agricultural systems and is usually thought of in that context. However, areas that can be maintained as meadows with tall, unmown grasses, such as Timothy, will provide excellent wildlife habitat. The grass is grazed by wildlife and rodents, and its seeds are consumed by birds. It provides areas for nesting, brooding, and foraging; cover for small mammals, game birds, and song birds; and habitat for insects. The tall, stiff stems may provide fall roosts for game birds. And with the addition of wildflowers and clovers in the unmown area, a nectar source for bees and butterflies is created along with colour and increased wildlife value.

Timothy is used in seed mixes for the rehabilitation of sites disturbed by construction. It helps stabilize the soil and is commonly used in some areas for erosion control.

Timothy seedlings may interfere with conifer seedling establishment by competing for resources, attracting insects and animals that consume conifer seeds, and producing toxins that interfere with conifer growth.

FERNS &
FERN ALLIES

The CLUB-MOSSES are an ancient group of plants that reproduce by spores. Today they are small and fairly inconspicuous plants, but 40 million years ago, lycophytes dominated major habitats as forest-forming trees more than 35 m tall. Club-mosses are usually evergreen, perennial, often trailing, and mostly temperate and subarctic. The leaves are simple, scale-like, and unlike those of any other plant. The spores are usually borne on a stalked cone-like structure that looks like a club. *Roland's Flora of Nova Scotia* lists 15 species of club mosses in four genera, including *Lycopodium*.

Family: Lycopodiaceae or Club-moss Family

HABITAT

Prefer shade to part-shade areas.

Thrive in acidic, organic soils.

Usually grow at the edges of fields and in roadside cuttings, disturbed ground, and dry, deciduous woods.

GENERAL COMMENTS

Club-mosses live in shady native plant communities in rich, organic soils. These communities provide a diverse ground cover. Club mosses have been used in the past as Christmas decorations, but their flammable spores make this increasingly rare.

FIELD HORSETAIL belongs to an ancient group of plants that grew as tall as trees during the Carboniferous Period. Now *Equisetum* is the only living genus, and its members are no more than 20 to 30 cm high.

Like the closely related ferns, horsetails have two types of stem. The dark-green sterile or vegetative stems are hollow, upright and jointed, bearing whorls of slender branches and tiny, toothed leaves at each node. The fertile (sport-bearing) stems lack chlorophyll and bear a cone at the tip. All horsetails are perennial, spreading by an extensive system of deep underground stems or rhizomes. Common Horsetail tolerates a wide range of conditions and is found throughout North America.

Family: Equisetaceae or Horsetail Family

Tolerates sun or shade.

Prefers wet to very dry, and acid to alkaline soils.

Usually grows in marshes, swamps, ditches, river banks, fields, and woods, and on roadsides and railroad embankments.

General Comments

Field Horsetail often forms dense stands, and due to its extensive belowground growth and ability to grow in sterile soils, it may effectively out-compete other types of vegetation. In agricultural systems it is considered a problematic weed that is difficult to control because it can re-sprout from its underground rhizomes and tubers, and because of its resistance to herbicides. It is considered toxic to some livestock, particularly horses.

Horsetail is also known as "scouring-rush" because its stems are structurally strengthened by silica grains. Early pioneers are reported to have used the plant to scour their pots and pans. The plants have also been used to polish metal and as fine sandpaper.

Water-horsetail (*E. fluviatile*) is commonly found in wet areas and may be used in pond or bog gardens in soil that is continually wet.

BRACKEN FERN is found throughout the world, except for hot and cold deserts. This large, coarse fern grows on a variety of soils and is an invasive succession species that is extremely competitive with other plants. The production and release of allelopathic (toxic) chemicals is also an important factor in its ability to dominate other vegetation. Bracken Fern contributes to potassium cycling in the ecosystem by effectively mobilizing phosphorus from inorganic sources. It spreads rapidly by its long, hairy rootstocks and forms large colonies. Bracken is often associated with birch, Sweetfern, and blueberry. It is the most common fern in Canada.

Family: Dennstaedtiacea

Toxicity: Known to be poisonous to livestock, causing thiamine deficiency in simple-stomach animals and acute toxicity in ruminants.

HABITAT

Prefers sunny areas but will tolerate shade.

Thrives in a variety of soils, but not waterlogged soils.

Succeeds on sites too dry for most ferns. Grows
best on deep, well-drained soils.

Commonly found in pastures, barrens, wasteland,
burnt-over areas, and roadsides.

Bracken is considered a troublesome weed in the agricultural and forestry industries. It is particularly difficult to control in blueberry fields, where soil cultivation is not practised. Its ability to produce allelopathic chemicals and its competitive capabilities make Bracken an unwanted plant in tree plantations, but desirable for discouraging tree invasion in areas where this is the desired land use. Bracken is useful in rehabilitation of disturbed sites and has been found to increase soil fertility by bringing nutrients into circulation through leaching from its bountiful litter. Its reproductive system is sensitive to acid rain.

Bracken provides cover and nesting sites for small mammals and birds. Bitter-tasting compounds, toxic chemicals and its poor palatability make its use as browse for wildlife uncommon. It is considered toxic to livestock, although it is occasionally browsed. Although several insect species feed on it, it is considered to be a potential source of insecticides.

Bracken was used as source of potash in the soap and glass industries in 1800s. The rhizomes have been used for tanning and to make a yellow dye. Dried and powdered it has been used as a flour in breads. In some areas of the world it is grown commercially for food and for herbal medicine. Several researchers have found all parts of Bracken to be mutagenic and carcinogenic in rodents.

CINNAMON FERN

CINNAMON FERN is one of the most common ferns in Nova Scotia. It reaches heights of less than 1 m. In early spring, the newly unrolling fronds have a woolly, light-brown covering that disappears as the pinnate fronds mature. In *Osmunda* species, spores form on modified fronds that emerge from the centre of the plant, start out bright green, and later turn a rich cinnamon brown. The rhizomes are stout, woody, creeping to sub-erect, and form dense mats.

Family: Osmundaceae or Royal Fern Family

HABITAT

Can tolerate both sun and shady areas.
Prefers moist acidic soils with high organic content.
Usually found in moist areas, wet marshy woods,
swamps, ditches, and on streambanks.

GENERAL COMMENTS

Cinnamon Fern has been widely cultivated as an ornamental for its beautiful cinnamon-coloured fertile fronds, its tall, vase-like shape, and its preference for partially shaded moist to wet areas.

HAY-SCENTED FERN

HAY-SCENTED FERN is a common native fern found throughout Nova Scotia. Named for the hay-like odour it emits when crushed, it can be identified by its lacy, light-green fronds, 25 to 35 cm long, which feel slightly sticky to the touch. It often grows in large colonies, forming a carpet, and spreads quickly by rhizomes.

Family: Dennstaedtiaceae

HABITAT

Prefers sunny areas.

Tolerates wide variation in environments.

Usually found in rocky or dry woodlands, dry hillsides and slopes, rock outcrops, pastures, clearings and roadsides.

GENERAL COMMENTS

Hay-scented Fern provides a beautiful, lacy, light-green cover on rocky, dry areas. Although native, under some conditions it behaves like an invasive species and forms dense stands by out-competing other species for nutritional and light resources and by its production of a thick mat of roots, which inhibit germination of other seed in the seed bank. It has been investigated for its allelopathic potential.

INTERRUPTED FERN

INTERRUPTED FERN is a large (1 m), deciduous native fern that can be distinguished from other ferns by the rust-coloured spore-bearing or fertile part of the fern, which is in the middle of otherwise sterile fronds. It propagates by spores and by rhizomes. Interrupted fern is found throughout the province and from Newfoundland to Manitoba, south to Missouri.

Family: Osmundaceae or Royal Fern Family

HABITAT

Prefers part shade to sun conditions.
Thrives in rich, fertile, neutral or somewhat acidic soils.
Usually found in damp fields or woods, moist thickets
   and margins of swamps.

GENERAL COMMENTS

Interrupted Fern is beautiful in woodland scenes and its spreading vase-like shape provides a pleasant background for colourful flowering plants in shade or part shade, or even full sun if the soil is moist. The fertile fronds, which appear halfway up infertile fronds, create the showy "interruption" that provides the common name.

NORTHERN LADY FERN

NORTHERN LADY FERN is a common species found throughout Nova Scotia. The fronds are lacy-looking, light green, almost 1 m long, 25 cm wide, and twice pinnate. A colonizer, it will grow in the cracks and crevices of rocks and even on bare soil. It frequently dominates on consistently wet soil and it may provide large-scale cover, but when growth is vigorous, it has been linked to soil instability on slopes.

Family: Dryopteridaceae or Wood Fern Family

HABITAT

Relatively tolerant of sun.

Moist, fertile, acidic soils and dry soil, but does best in sun if soil is moist.

Usually found on roadsides, pastures, borders of woods and in thickets.

GENERAL COMMENTS

This native perennial fern is beautiful where it naturally occurs and can be used in woodland gardens. With its delicate, lacy look, its arching fronds, and continually added new leaves, Northern Lady Fern maintains a lush look throughout the growing season. It tolerates dryer soils than many ferns.

ROYAL FERN

ROYAL FERN is from the same family (Osmundaceae) as fossils dating back 230 million years, and is found on all continents except Australia. Its branching resembles a small tree, and it grows to almost 2 m. The pinnules are separate and attached to the main branch by a short stem; the fertile parts are borne on the main branch. The fern spreads by rhizomes just below the soil surface. The rhizomes are clothed in roots that act as a protective armour and nutrient transporter. The fern is quite unique in that the spores, which are released in spring/early summer, are viable for only two days then die; spores from other ferns remain viable for years. This fern occupies large areas of southwestern Nova Scotia, and is common throughout the province.

Family: Osmundaceae or Royal Fern Family

HABITAT

Tolerant of sun to shade areas.

Prefers moist soils.

Commonly found in wet ditches, streams and rivers, bogs, and at the edges of wet woods.

GENERAL COMMENTS

The attractive, feathery foliage of this bold, robust fern make it a noticeable plant. In bogs or along ponds, with flowers and grasses, it provides cover and protection for reptiles and amphibians, and and mammals eat the young fiddleheads in spring.

SENSITIVE FERN

SENSITIVE FERN is a native fern found throughout eastern Canada and the United States, and west to Manitoba. It is a good colonizer and often the first species to grow in disturbed moist areas. It spreads by long creeping rhizomes into dense colonies; large patches can be seen on our roadsides. The fronds are light green and 30 to 50 cm high. Sensitive Fern dies back quickly with the first frost, leaving the erect fertile spikes visible.

Family: Dryopteridaceae or Wood Fern Family

HABITAT

Tolerant of part sun to shade areas.
Prefers damp or wet areas with neutral to slightly acid soils.
Usually found in marshes, roadside ditches, and
   other wet areas.

GENERAL COMMENTS

Sensitive Fern is a low-growing, low-maintenance fern for moist sites such as bogs, pond edges, and seepages. The erect, brownish reproductive spikes are showy when the foliage dies down at the first frost. Sensitive Fern is tough and spreads quickly to form colonies. It is reported to be toxic to wildlife and is not browsed by deer, but it does provide cover for reptiles, amphibians, and small mammals.

LICHENS & BRYOPHYTES

LICHENS

There are thousands of species of lichens, from the tropics to polar regions. In the U.S. and Canada alone, there are probably more than 3600 species. They grow on tree bark, rocks and soil, and in some of the most inhospitable places on earth.

Each lichen is actually a symbiotic association between a fungus and green alga or a cyanobacterium. The fungus protects the alga from dessication and absorbs nutrients from the surface. The alga synthesizes organic nutrients and nitrogen-rich compounds that help support the fungal partner.

Lichens can be categorized into three broad groups: *Corticolous* lichens are found on tree bark and dead bark, *saxicolous* lichens on rocks, and *terricolous* lichens colonize soil.

Lichens play vital roles as soil stabilizers and in nutrient cycling for other plants. The cyanobacteria that live with and around them are able to "fix" atmospheric nitrogen and make it available to other plants—a major source of nitrogen in many native ecosystems. As lichens grow, they break down rocks by excreting acids, and help create soil.

Lichens obtain their nutrients from rainwater. This makes them very sensitive to air pollution. When pollution-tolerant species thrive, it indicates deteriorating air quality. Lichens are also extremely vulnerable to habitat disturbance, so the most diverse lichen communities are found where there has been little disturbance. As a result, they are used as bioindicators to monitor both air quality and ecosystem health.

Lichens provide food for invertebrates; larger animals browse on them; and some birds use lichens for nest-building material. Lichens have been used as dyes and as medicines. It is estimated that about 50 percent of all lichen species have antibiotic qualities. In addition, many species provide colour, texture and form to the natural landscape.

Lichens are widespread in Nova Scotia and are major components of biological diversity in many habitats, including soil crusts. They are frequently seen in extensive mats on roadside rocks and soils, often in association with mosses.

Four species commonly found on our roadsides are described on the following pages.

Cladonia cristatella Tuck.

BRITISH SOLDIER has a broken, scalelike base that bears a number of erect hollow standards, which terminate in bright-red fruiting bodies. The common name presumably refers to the red "uniform." A very common species, British Soldier is the lichen most likely to attract the attention of the casual observer. It grows on the ground or on dead wood and can tolerate severe conditions that are unfavorable to most other plants. High humidity, low light intensities and cool temperatures are favorable for their growth; moisture is the most critical factor. The algal partner is *Pleurococcus*, a green alga often found on the bark of trees.

HABITAT

Prefers shade to part shade.
Primarily colonizes soil, particularly poor soil, and
    rocks and dead wood.
Common everywhere.

DOG LICHEN or FELT LICHEN

Peltigera canina (L.) Willd.

DOG LICHEN is a terricolous lichen found on infertile roadside soils. It can fix considerable amounts of nitrogen, making it an important component of nutrient cycling in these infertile soils.

HABITAT

Grows best in full sun but can tolerate shade.
Tolerant of shallow, sterile soil.
Adapted to cooler climates.
Found growing on soil, rock, humus, moss, and fallen logs.

GREY-GREEN REINDEER MOSS

REINDEER MOSS is a terricolous lichen found on moist to dry, nitrogen-deficient soil and on rocks, and is an important winter feed for caribou in northern Canada. It is slow growing, long lived, densely branched, and forms large greyish-white colonies or mats under conditions unfavourable for other plants. Reindeer Moss has a wider ecological range than other reindeer lichens, and is more common than others in less-favorable habitats including wet bogs and shaded woods.

HABITAT

Tolerant of shade and sun.

Prefers moist to acidic, dry, sandy, nitrogen-poor soils on a shallow humus layer or peat.

PINK EARTH or CAP LICHEN

Dibaeis baeomyces (L.F.) Rawbold Hertel

PINK EARTH is a mushroom-shaped lichen, 1-3 mm high, named for the pinkish tinge of the large colonies it forms on bare soil. It is common on roadsides on disturbed soils. It can be considered a pioneer species, providing cover and thus reducing erosion.

HABITAT

Tolerant of sun and shade.
Colonizes soil.
Usually found along clay banks and roadsides.

Bryophyte is the collective name given to mosses and liverworts, which are believed to have evolved from green algae, and were the first land-based green plants.

There are over 400 native species of mosses in Nova Scotia, occupying many different habitats. Species commonly found on rocks, in pastures, along streams, and on bare soil, and are found in these habitats when they occur along roadsides.

Mosses play an important role in nutrient-poor ecosystems. They lack true stems, leaves, and roots, though they may have parts that resemble these structures. They absorb the nutrients and minerals they need from the air and from what is washed off the foliage of higher plants. Some can survive long periods of dry weather because their structure allows them to absorb moisture very quickly and revive. Mosses reproduce through a process known as alternation of generations; the familiar capsules on long stalks (the sporophytes) release spores.

Although these native plants are small and inconspicuous, they are adapted to almost every habitat and play major roles in native ecosystems in Nova Scotia. They are resilient and successful. They are able to survive periods of drought, and they provide a soil cover on nutrient-poor sites, including cut slopes resulting from construction. Eventually they provide a continuing source of organic matter to soils, and they function as sediment filters. They intercept and absorb moisture and nutrients from precipitation. Since they accumulate chemical elements, they can be used as indicators of air and water pollution. They play important roles in water and nutrient cycling and in relationships with other plants and with animals. They provide food and habitat for many invertebrates, and nesting materials for birds.

HABITATS

Woodlands, forest floor, tree trunks and branches, stumps, swamps, bogs, ditches, running water, disturbed soil, roadsides, rocks, and grassy areas.

FIRE MOSS

Ceratodon spp.

FIRE MOSS is a short, native moss that forms dense tufts or cushions with stalks up to 2.5 cm and a spore capsule on the tip. Often found on disturbed sites on a wide range of soils, it rapidly colonizes these soils and prevents soil loss through erosion. It is often found associated with Fireweed and Pearly Everlasting. An abundance of Fire Moss promotes a large accumulation of organic matter. It can tolerate higher pollution levels than other mosses.

HAIR CAP MOSS

HAIR CAP MOSS is a larger moss with coarse "leaves." The spore capsules look like boxes with four flat sides and are borne on a tall stalk. This moss is generally pollution-tolerant. It is commonly found in fields, creating hummocks, and in marshes and rocky woods.

Hair Cap Moss with fruiting capsules

SOIL CRUSTS

Biological SOIL CRUSTS are complex mosaics of living organisms, including algae, cyanobacteria (blue-green algae), bacteria, lichens, mosses, liverworts, and fungi. They generally grow in semi-arid to arid climates on or just below the soil surface on shrub land, grassland, and open woodland.

Biological soil crusts are different from chemical and physical crusts, such as salt crusts, because they do not create a hard impermeable surface. They help stabilize soil; some organisms even excrete a sticky substance that helps bind particles together. They improve soil fertility and are productive even during cooler temperatures thereby increasing the time organic carbon remains in the soil. Certain soil crusts can improve soil moisture by increasing roughness, therefore increasing infiltration. In addition, some types can fix nitrogen.

By destroying these crusts, ATVs, hikers, vehicles, and construction can increase soil erosion by 50 percent, even when vegetation damage is not apparent. Disturbance can also reduce plant health by decreasing soil fertility. Overall, soil crusts provide many soil improvements, thus encouraging native species to germinate and proliferate.

UNDESIRABLE PLANTS

NOXIOUS WEEDS
&
NUISANCE PLANTS

INTRODUCTION

UNDESIRABLE PLANTS are, by definition, plants that are not wanted where they are growing. They may be classed in two categories:

• NOXIOUS WEEDS: invasive species that are highly destructive to agricultural and other environments and difficult to control.
• NUISANCE PLANTS: invasive species that interfere with human activities but are not considered devastating enough to be classified as noxious.

Some weeds are potentially more devastating to society than others and are listed in weed-control laws. In Nova Scotia, noxious weeds are classified under the Weed Control Act as either Class Number One or Class Number Two. See the next page for a list.

WHAT TO DO ABOUT UNDESIRABLE PLANTS

Know the biology of the plant. Find out how it spreads (by underground roots and stems or by seed), and whether it is annual, biennial, or perennial.

1. Detect weeds before they have a chance to spread
Correct identification is essential since sometimes only subtle differences distinguish them from similar or closely related plants that are not considered harmful.

2. Remove them
Pull out by the roots if possible, or cut off at ground level if you cannot get at the roots. Leave the tops on the ground if no flowers or seeds are present. Otherwise, bag the tops and remove them from the site, taking care to dispose of them where their seeds or roots cannot re-establish new populations. In many cases, seeds remain in the soil and new plants continue to crop up.

3. Don't grow them
Be careful not to bring in root fragments, seeds, or rooted sections of noxious or invasive plants. Monitor disturbed areas to make sure none of these plants take root.

LIST OF NOXIOUS WEEDS IN NOVA SCOTIA

DEFINITION: Weeds listed in the weed control regulations under the Weed Control Act. The list below was current in 2003.

CLASS NUMBER ONE

Weeds capable of spreading to cultivated or pasture lands by:
- wind-borne seeds
- seed dispersal by birds, animals, water, or other
- vines and roots across property boundaries.

Common Name	Scientific Name	Area
Field Bindweed	*Convolvulus arvensis* L.	Province
Marsh Hedge Nettle	*Stachys palustris* L.	Province
Leafy Spurge	*Euphorbia esula* L.	Province
Common Milkweed	*Asclepias syriaca* L.	Province
Yellow Nut Sedge	*Cyperus esculentus* L.	Province
Tansy Ragwort	*Senecio jacobaea* L.	Western and Central
White Cockle	*Lychnis alba* Mill.	Province
Velvetleaf	*Abutilon theophrasti* Medik.	Province
Coltsfoot	*Tussilago farfara* L.	Province
Wild Chervil	*Anthriscus sylvestris* Hoffm.	Province
Blue Weed	*Echium vulgare* L.	Province

CLASS NUMBER TWO

Weeds capable of inflicting economic loss or ill health on people within the province.

Common Name	Scientific Name	Area
Poison Ivy	*Rhus* spp.	Province
Ragweed	*Ambrosia* spp.	Province
Jimsonweed	*Datura* spp.	Province
Stinging Nettle	*Urtica* spp.	Province

The next pages describe three species from Nova Scotia's 2003 noxious weed list as well as two nuisance species.

Nova Scotia's Weed Control Regulations are available at:
www.gov.ns.ca/just/regulations/regs/wcontrol.htm

A complete list of identification factsheets about Nova Scotia's noxious weeds is available at:
www.gov.ns.ca/nsaf/rir/weeds/noxious.htm

COLTSFOOT is one of the earliest plants to flower in spring. The bright-yellow flower heads of this perennial from Europe look a lot like dandelions, but they appear before the leaves. The flower stalks are also distinctive, being covered in pink scales and a white fluff like that on asparagus stems. Each seed has a tuft of fluffy hair at the top that allows it to be transported by the wind. The round or heart-shaped leaves are smooth on top and woolly beneath, and have large teeth on their margins.

Family: Asteraceae or Aster Family

HABITAT

Prefers full sun but tolerates partial shade.

Thrives in cool, damp soils with a high clay content.

Usually found on cliffs and stream banks, and on gravelly areas, including roadside shoulders, where the soil has been disturbed.

NOXIOUS WEED: CONTROL

Coltsfoot can infest large areas in a short time. It spreads by seed but primarily by rhizome—up to 10 m each year. Coltsfoot is currently under review to remove it from the noxious weed list.

RAGWEED

RAGWEED is a common cause of hayfever, and may be found in many places in Nova Scotia. Its fernlike, deeply lobed leaves are opposite at the base of the plant, alternate closer to the top of the plant, and covered with fine hairs. The plant grows to 50 cm but will adapt to mowing, producing flowers and seeds close to the ground. In August and September numerous green male flower heads are borne in clusters at the top of the plant; the female flower heads grow in the axils of the upper leaves.

Ragweed is an annual plant. It produces a large quantity of pollen, causing allergy problems for humans, and its numerous seeds can remain viable for more than 40 years. Ragweed is toxic to livestock, causing nausea, and it imparts an unpleasant odor to dairy products produced from cows allowed to graze on it. It outcompetes other plants because it rapidly absorbs many nutrients and trace metals from the soil, causing nutrient deficiencies in surrounding plants.

Family: Asteraceae or Aster Family

Prefers full sun.

Tolerant of different soils; particularly thrives in loamy soils with a pH between 6 and 7. It is very tolerant of salt conditions.

Usually found on roadsides, waste areas, and fields.

Noxious Weed: Control

Ragweed can be controlled mechanically through mowing or by pulling out the plant before it flowers. Seed production must be prevented for long-term control.

TANSY RAGWORT or STINKING WILLIE

TANSY RAGWORT is an erect biennial or perennial from Europe. Its stems are branched and woolly near the top, its leaves deeply lobed into irregular segments and irregularly toothed. In the first year the plant produces a rosette of leaves 5 to 30 cm wide; in the second, a tall flower stem up to 1 m in height. The golden-yellow flowers form flat-topped clusters at the ends of the branches from July to September. Tansy Ragwort produces numerous seeds, which remain viable for many years. It also reproduces from small root fragments, making the plant very difficult to control.

Tansy Ragwort is found throughout Nova Scotia—especially in Pictou east to northern Cape Breton—and is becoming common in Colchester and Cumberland counties. It is very toxic to livestock, especially horses and cattle, causing a group of diseases called seneciosis, for which there is no treatment. These undesirable qualities make this a noxious weed.

Family: Asteraceae or Aster Family

Prefers sunny conditions.

Thrives in disturbed, well-drained soil but can adapt to other conditions.

It commonly grows on roadsides, pastures, clearings and waste places.

Noxious Weed: Control

Tansy Ragwort can be controlled by mowing the plant before it flowers, and through biological control. Cinnabar Moth is the most common biological control; its larvae feed on leaves, buds, and flowers. Other biological controls include Ragwort Flea Beetle and a root-feeding moth, both of which have been released in Nova Scotia.

JAPANESE KNOTWEED

JAPANESE KNOTWEED is an agressive introduced invasive weed that can reach heights of 2.5 m. It forms dense thickets of reddish, branching, hollow (except at nodes) stems that resemble bamboo, smothering all other vegetation. This perennial species is difficult to control because of its vigorous spreading rhizomes, which form a deep, dense mat. The inconspicuous, whitish flowers are borne in open, drooping panicles. It rarely establishes from seed, usually spreading by re-sprouting from fragments.

Family: Polygonaceae or Buckwheat Family

HABITAT

Prefers sun to part shade.

Thrives on moist, well-drained, nutrient rich soil.

Usually found in waste places, neglected gardens, and storm drains, along streambanks, and on roadsides.

NUISANCE PLANT: CONTROL

Japanese Knotweed is extremely difficult to eradicate once established, regardless of where it is found. It was once culti-vated as an edible plant, but it is now generally considered a nuisance. In some areas, the plant is reported to be a fire haz-ard in its dormant season.

PURPLE LOOSESTRIFE

Lythrum salicaria L.

Purple Loosestrife is a native of Europe. Its six-petaled magenta flowers are borne on slender spikes that bloom from June to September. The leaves are stalkless, with hairs on the stems. Purple Loosestrife is very invasive, choking out native plants in wetlands degrading food, shelter, and nesting sites for wildlife. Currently it is being monitored throughout the province and control methods are being researched.

Family: Lythraceae or Loosetrife Family

HABITAT

Prefers sun to part shade.
Thrives in wet soils.
Prefers marshes, ditches, and low ground throughout the province.

NUISANCE PLANT: CONTROL

Although Purple Loosestrife's gorgeous flowers make a beautiful showing in ditches and marshes, it is of ecological concern because of its invasive nature. Although infestations appear to spread more slowly here than out west or further south, biological control agents have been released on many Purple Loosestrife populations in Nova Scotia. Effort should be taken to avoid growing or spreading it.

RESTORATION TECHNIQUES

USING PLANTS: from home gardens to ecological restoration

INTRODUCTION

This book was originally written as a guide for those involved in restoring roadside habitat in Nova Scotia, usually after construction. The intent was to encourage an ecological approach, with an emphasis on healthy soil and native plants. Indeed, even large-scale drainage and slope problems can be tackled using native plant material harvested with no lasting impact on the environment.

In the hope that they will find a wider audience, many of the original fact sheets have been retained in this edition. Whatever the source of disturbance, and however small the area, the techniques described on the following pages will help speed the return to a more natural habitat. Missing, however, are the references to large-scale projects and machinery contained in the first edition.

NOVA SCOTIA

During the Pleistocene or Ice Age, glaciers eliminated all vegetation from Nova Scotia. Our current flora consists of plants that began expanding their populations into Nova Scotia only ten thousand years ago. Today the province is a transition zone. Many plant species reached us from the northeastern United States; others are part of Canada's mighty boreal forest. Our vegetation also includes many herbaceous species imported from elsewhere through human activity.

Our soil, too, has had only ten thousand years to develop. Most of the parent material is glacial till closely related to the underlying bedrock. In general, our soils are infertile and slightly to strongly acidic, except in areas high in limestone or gypsum, where the pH is higher.

RESTORING HABITAT

To restore natural habitats and functioning ecosystems to newly disturbed areas, it is first essential to identify what plants grow naturally in the region, and to learn about their specific environmental requirements. The key is to start with an understanding of the importance of soil biology. Working with whatever soil is available, the next step is to add compost if necessary, stabilize the area by seeding with a ground cover of grasses and legumes, and then over time to reestablish the desired local native community using wildflower seeds, transplants, hardwood cuttings, and natural regrowth.

PURPOSE

- Start with the basics, a healthy soil
- Use biology to encourage the growth of native species
- Establish vegetation quickly

SOIL FOOD WEB

- Each type of plant community has its own unique soil food web
- A community of organisms: bacteria, algae, fungi, protozoa, insects, arthropods, earthworms, small vertebrates, and plants
- Result of soil, climate, vegetation and land management
- Starts with sunlight: lichens, mosses, algae, and higher plants use photosynthesis to make food
- Plant by-products and residues feed soil organisms
- Organisms decompose organic matter, store plant nutrients, fix atmospheric nitrogen, enhance soil porosity (which increases infiltration and reduces runoff), and become food for higher organisms

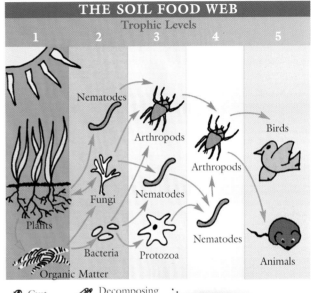

THE SOIL FOOD WEB

Trophic Levels

1   2   3   4   5

Nematodes

Arthropods

Arthropods

Birds

Fungi

Nematodes

Plants

Bacteria

Protozoa

Nematodes

Animals

Organic Matter

Cyst

Protozoa

Organic matter

Bacteria

Decomposing plant cells

Nematodes

Spores

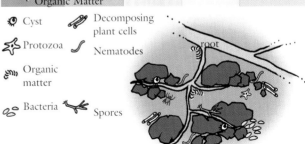

root

ADVANTAGES OF HEALTHY SOIL

- A healthy soil supports plant growth and protects water quality
- Biological activity and diversity increase
- As diversity and productivity increase, need for fertilizer decreases
- Water infiltration increases
- Organisms degrade pollutants
- Soil loss ceases
- Disease suppression increases
- Site management may alter composition of organisms intentionally or unintentionally

BACTERIA IN SOIL

- Role: decompose organic matter, keep nutrients where roots are, improve soil structure, degrade pollutants, and improve water infiltration and water-holding capacity through aggregates
- Bacteria fix atmospheric nitrogen in a symbiotic association with the roots of legumes and some native shrubs
- Nitrifying bacteria are suppressed in forest soils
- Actinomycetes decompose hard-to-degrade substrates and are active at high pHs
- Important in newly disturbed soil for vegetation to establish

FUNGI IN SOIL

- Grow as long threads in soil (hyphae)
- Decompose hard-to-degrade substrates at low pHs
- Increase accumulation of organic material
- Retain nutrients; reduce leaching
- Bind soil particles into aggregates that increase water-holding capacity
- Mycorrhizal fungi associate with the roots of many plants and increase their ability to access moisture and nutrients

Poorly quality soil requires improvement to grow plants

ARTHROPODS IN SOIL

- Forest soils have more arthropods than earthworms
- Typical arthropods are insects (springtails, ants, beetles), arachnids (spiders, mites), crustaceans (sowbugs), and centipedes and millipedes
- Improve soil structure and increase soil aggregation
- Stimulate microorganism activity by shredding organic material to make it more accessible for those organisms
- A m^3 of soil may contain from 500 to more than 200,000 arthropods, depending on the soil, plants, and management activities on the site

EARTHWORMS IN SOIL

- Grassy soils have more earthworms than arthropods, in contrast to forest soils
- Improve water infiltration and water-holding capacity; minimize runoff and erosion
- Also enhance activity of microorganisms, increase nutrient cycling, and open channels for root growth

RATIO OF BACTERIA TO FUNGI

- Characteristic of type of ecosystem: bacteria dominate grass systems; fungi dominate forest ecosystems
- Fungal biomass higher in forest soils, affecting pH, nitrogen, and nutrient retention
- Bacteria use simple organic compounds; fungi use complex compounds
- Management practices can change the bacteria:fungi ratio
- May be possible to alter species composition on a site by manipulating the bacteria:fungi ratio
- Can change the ratio and the plant species depending on the type of organic matter added to the soil. Woody materials increase fungi

USING TOPSOIL AND SOIL SEED BANKS

PURPOSE

- Restore native vegetation to a disturbed site
- Enhance natural dispersal of native plants (wild flowers and shrubs)
- Establish species-rich vegetation
- Eliminate problems with collecting, storing, seeding and transplanting desirable species

DONOR SEED BANKS

- Identify nearby sources of desirable plant material
- Donor soils provide seed, root propagules, plant nutrients, appropriate soil structure and chemistry, and micro-organisms
- Identify the desirable and unwanted species in that area
- Should have no or very few unwanted species
- Characterize the growth habits and environmental needs for each dominant species
- Identify soil moisture and temperature requirements for germination of desired species

Topsoil (donor soil) pushed and stored at top of slope to be reused.

USING DONOR SOIL

- Remove donor soil (topsoil) to re-use for re-vegetation
- Beginning of growing season is best time to remove it
- If possible, use it immediately
- Store donor soil for as short a time as possible and preferably in small heaps
- Spread donor soil as topsoil 5 to 7 cm thick on area to be vegetated
- If area is not likely to be mowed, some woody debris may be left
- Soil bank will have seeds and root pieces of desirable and undesirable vegetation if both were present before removal
- May also use donor soil as light topdressing on other soils to provide seed and soil organisms

ALTERING ON-SITE ENVIRONMENT

- Manipulate environmental conditions to reduce undesirable species
- Manipulate to optimize desirable species
- Moisture, fertilizer, organic matter, and pH may be altered to help determine species that will germinate and grow on the site

USING COMPOST

WHEN MIXED WITH SOIL OR AS TOPDRESSING
- Source of plant nutrients
- Improves soil structure
- Increases moisture retention

EROSION CONTROL FOR LARGER AREAS
- Berms on slopes to decrease runoff and sediment loss
- Blanket on slopes to slow runoff
- Flow check in ditches
- Replaces silt fences of geotextile

MIXED WITH SOIL
- Blend 20 to 25% by volume with poor-quality soil to 'manufacture' topsoil
- Enhances water- and nutrient-holding capacity, soil structure, organic matter, and drainage
- Use only where type of vegetation requires fertility

AS TOPDRESSING ON POORLY VEGETATED GRASSY SITES
- To produce dense sod on cut slopes
- Provides beneficial microorganisms
- Provides plant nutrients
- Increases moisture retention for vegetation
- Increases the size and vitality of each plant on the site

COMPOST ANALYSIS
- Know the nutrient content of the compose
- Some composts may have few major plant nutrients, but will still improve soil characteristics
- Some native plants require high organic matter but low-nutrient soil
- Low-nutrient compost may serve the same purpose as peat
- Product must meet CCME guidelines
- Facilities in Nova Scotia must meet Department of Environment and Labour Guidelines

PURPOSE

- Improve seedling establishment by altering micro-climate
- Inhibit competing vegetation
- Suppress weeds
- Prevent water loss from soil through evaporation
- Insulate soil and moderate soil temperatures
- Prevent crusting of soil surface
- Improve infiltration of water into soil
- Prevent splash erosion
- May add nutrients to soil
- May prevent frost heaving of new plants.

APPLICATION

- Landscape fabric may be used under mulches
- A layer 5–10 cm deep is usually sufficient

STRAW

- Generally seed free, although may be grain seeds
- Clean and dry
- Disadvantage: may shift during windy conditions

WOOD CHIPS

- Clean and dry, but may be difficult to apply by hand
- No seeds introduced to site

BARK

- Most widely used mulch material for landscape plantings
- Moist and heavy to handle
- No seeds introduced to site
- If using wheelbarrow, try a manure fork, which works far better than a shovel

HAY

- May use old or fresh hay
- If old, may be mouldy, a potential respiratory problem
- May provide wildflower seed if hay is from run-down fields
- Provides locally adapted seed from hay-field grasses
- Disadvantage: may supply undesirable 'weed' seeds and may shift during windy conditions.

INTRODUCING PLANTS TO THE SITE

PURPOSE

- Cover bare soil to stabilize and prevent erosion
- Protect drainage areas, streambanks and shorelines
- Protect slopes from erosion
- Provide visually attractive scene
- Provide habitat for beneficial insects, birds, and wildlife
- Protect site from invading unwanted vegetation
- Provide wind, snow, and visual barriers

METHODS

- Utilizing native soils found onsite as root and seed banks
- Seeding
- Transplanting clumps of native plant communities
- Transplanting rooted plants propagated from onsite or nearby
- Direct insertion of hardwood cuttings of native shrubs
- Use of bioengineering techniques

SOIL AMENDMENTS

PURPOSE OF PRODUCTS

- Change characteristics of soil
- Provide plant nutrients for seedlings or transplants
- Enhance plant establishment and growth
- Manage soil moisture

FERTILIZER (PLANT NUTRIENTS)

- Needed after seeds germinate for maximum growth
- High nitrogen in spring and summer, low in fall
- Fertilizer rates according to soil test

COMPOST

- Compost mixed into soil, 20 to 25% by volume, may replace fertilizer
- Compost provides many advantages over chemical fertilizers
- Several types of compost with variable plant nutrients depending on feed stocks

INOCULATES

- Bacterial inoculates for legumes, such as clovers, may be necessary for nitrogen fixing
- Mycorrhizal fungi improve ability of some plants to utilize soil resources

LIME

- Lime to be used only when pH is below 6.0
- Add lime only when desired vegetation requires non-acidic soil
- Some native plants require acidic soils
- Many grasses and legumes need neutral soils to thrive

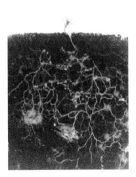

Pine seedling with extensive root system and white filaments of mycorrhizal fungus. Mycorrhizae dramatically increase amount of soil plant can use.

SEEDING SEED MIXES

PURPOSE

- Provide vegetation cover to stabilize disturbed and bare soils
- Reduce erosion and prevent soil loss
- Increase water infiltration
- Provide favourable sites for later species
- Provide attractive ground cover
- Provide habitat

EFFECTS OF DENSE GRASS/CLOVER STAND

- Ongoing prevention of soil loss
- 70 to 80% vegetative cover will control erosion
- Protection from extremes for succeeding species (shade, moisture)
- Very dense, no space for succeeding species (e.g., woody)
- Increases frost damage to young tree seedlings
- Increases fertility of soil
- Helps establish soil microflora and microfauna, which play roles in nutrient cycling and disease suppression
- Builds up soils with addition of organic matter; contributes to topsoil development

*Example of good and
attractive cover.
(A mixture of Birds-foot
Trefoil, various grasses
and Cat-tail)*

RECLAMATION SEED MIXES FOR LARGE AREAS

- Nova Scotia Highway Seed Mix
- Devco Tailing Mix with Birdsfoot-trefoil
- Prince Edward Island Highway Seed Mix
- New Brunswick Highway Seed Mix
- Other reclamation mixes (with a nitrogen-fixing legume)

FACTORS IN SEED MIX SELECTION

- Native species are not available commercially and are too costly to collect
- Seed mixes should meet short-term and long-term objectives
- May need different seed mixes for different site conditions and objectives
- Mixes must germinate and establish quickly (in variable soil and climate conditions)
- Grasses usually balanced between sod-forming species and bunch grasses, with legumes added for their nitrogen-fixing abilities
- Sod-forming species may inhibit the growth of woody plants; Creeping Red Fescue is an aggressive sod former

SEEDING RATES

- Rates are designed to provide sufficient seed for purposes but not too much to cause competition
- Purity, germination percentages and seed weights necessary to formulate mix

SEEDING DATES AND MOISTURE

- Two weeks of moisture needed for germination and early establishment
- Early spring to early June and mid-August to mid-September are the best times in Nova Scotia
- Summer seeding requires irrigation or specialized product to retain moisture
- Late-summer seeding may not provide enough cover to stabilize soil over winter

SEEDING WILDFLOWERS

PURPOSE

- To introduce local wildflowers for colour and variety
- To introduce economically

SOURCES OF SEED

- No locally collected or grown wildflower seed is commercially available in Nova Scotia
- Commercially available seed may not be adapted to this climate
- Most commercial seed originates from the west coast; even though wild flower is native to North America, the source is a different ecotype
- May be introduced on a site as 'hay' from a local source

WILDFLOWER SPECIES TO COLLECT

- Know the plants: you must be able to identify the plants you wish to collect
- Distinguish between native (present before European settlement) and naturalized (exotic or alien) species
- Native species: Goldenrods, Asters, Pearly Everlasting, Joe-pye-weed, Boneset, Fireweed
- Naturalized species: Yarrow, Ox-eye Daisy, Hawkweeds, Wild Carrot, Birdsfoot-trefoil, Ragged Robin, Black-eyed Susan, Rabbitfoot Clover
- Avoid agricultural weeds and nuisance plants
- Do not collect or spread Sweet Clovers, Purple Loosestrife or any species on noxious weed list
- Lupine may be introduced by seed, but is spreading on its own, so not recommended for further introductions

COLLECTING WILDFLOWER SEED

- Wild populations of naturalized and plentiful native species can be collected on a sustained-yield basis
- Timing of seed collection: For some species the window for collecting is small (two weeks); for others it can be longer (three to four months)
- Collect when seed is nearly mature; immature seeds have reduced viability
- Collect from healthy plants with no evidence of disease
- Whenever possible, collect after seed has begun to disperse naturally
- Collect no more than 50% of the seed of each plant
- Collect no more than 10% from a population in an area
- Leave majority to assure the continuation of the species at that location
- Do not collect from the same location annually; rotate collecting locations to minimize impact on the population
- Always ask landowner's permission

[ABOVE] Commercial wildflower-mix trials. End of first season's growth. Most of these did not persist.

[LEFT] One of the few species that persisted for 3 years.

RARE SPECIES

- Be aware of potential rare plants in area and laws protecting them
- Rare plants grow within a limited range or in specialized habitats
- Rare plants can, however, be plentiful in their preferred habitat

HOW TO INTRODUCE TO A SITE

- Small quantities may be spread by hand in early spring, or at time of their natural dispersal
- Make sure site and soil conditions are appropriate for species being introduced

AFTER COLLECTING

- When transporting seeds from the collection site keep them cool; high temperatures can reduce viability of seeds
- Use a paper bag or perforated plastic bag to store the seeds after collecting
- Keep seeds in a cool, dry, protected place before cleaning
- Seeds do not have to be cleaned before storage, but it is a good idea

CLEANING SEEDS

- Cleaning separates flower parts from the seed and makes it easier to store and sow the seeds
- Separate seeds from flowers by rubbing a handful between hands or shaking vigorously in a bag
- Sift seeds from rest of floral parts by using sieves of different sizes, or
- Separate seeds by allowing a light breeze to blow away the lighter chaff

STORAGE

- Store seeds in a fridge set at 1 to 5°C for several months or until ready to sow
- Seeds of wetland plants need to be kept for several months in cold, damp conditions to mimic winter

WOODY PLANT PROPAGATION

PURPOSE

- To expand the population and density of desirable shrubs on a site
- To introduce desirable species to a site
- To produce containerized plants for transplanting

NATIVE PLANTS EASILY PROPAGATED BY STEM CUTTINGS

- Willows (*Salix* spp.)
- Red Osier Dogwood (*Cornus sericea*)
- Meadowsweet (*Spiraea latifolia*)
- Steeplebush (*Spirea tomentosa*)
- Wild Rose (*Rosa virginiana*)
- Bayberry (*Myrica pensylvanica*)
- Canada Holly (*Ilex verticillata*)
- Wild Raisin (*Viburnum nudum*)
- Highbush Cranberry (*Viburnum opulus*)
- Bush Honeysuckle (*Diervilla lonicera*)
- Black-berried Elder (*Sambucus canadensis*)

COLLECTION OF STEM CUTTINGS

- Collect from accessible site, with reasonable population of the desired plants
- Collect in spring, after first flush of growth
- Parent plants should have vigorously growing stems and be in good health with no disease or insect infestation
- Cuttings are taken from upper branches of young, healthy plants with a sharp tool to give smooth, clean cut
- Do not collect more than 20% from any plant nore more than 20% from population
- Collect a few from several plants to maintain genetic diversity
- Must be kept cool and moist from field to propagating area

1 Use cuttings that are 6 to 12 cm long, stripping off the leaves and side twigs from the bottom 3 to 8 cm of the stem

2 Dip the bottom end of the cutting in No.1 rooting powder, tap off excess and place cutting in rooting medium (mixture of perlite and peat moss or perlite and vermiculite)

3 Keep the propagating bed moist, with high humidity, by covering with white plastic.

4 When cutting is well rooted, transplant into individual pots with suitable growing medium and place in the shade to grow

[RIGHT] Rooted stem cutting ready to transplant into pots.

NATIVE PLANTS PROPAGATED BY ROOT CUTTINGS

- Sweetfern (*Comptonia peregrina*)

COLLECTION OF ROOT CUTTINGS

- Collect from accessible site, with reasonable population of Sweetfern plants
- Collect in November/December after several hard frosts, so plants are dormant
- Dig up plants, cut off long pieces of roots with sharp knife and keep moist
- Cut the end closest to the plant with a straight cut

PREPARING THE ROOT CUTTINGS

1 Cut the roots into 5-cm sections and lay them horizontally on the rooting medium (mix of perlite and peat moss) about 2 to 3 cm apart
2 Cover lightly with 1 to 2 cm of rooting medium
3 Keep moist but not excessively wet by covering with plastic and place in cold during the winter
4 In spring/summer after top growth is vigorous and there is a lot of root growth, transplant into growing medium in individual pots and place in shade to grow

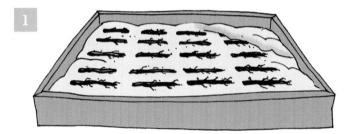

1

Rooted root cutting of Sweetfern that was collected in early November. (Photo taken the end of following summer)

GROWING TO TRANSPLANT SIZE

- Keep plants growing with regular applications of liquid fertilizer
- Plants may be transplanted onto the site in late fall
- If overwintering in pots, keep sheltered and cold
- Transplant in early spring

TRANSPLANTING AT THE SITE

- Plants should be thoroughly fertilized before transplanting onto sites
- Transplant very early in the spring, or in the fall
- Holes may be dug for 10-cm pots by pulling out chunk of soil with a mattock and placing transplant in hole
- Firm the soil around the transplant
- Record location, species, dates, and any other relevant information

Greenhouse facility outside technical services at Miller Lake (greenhouse constructed using salvaged materials).

Interior showing automatic irrigation system and summer shading.

PLANTING OF HARDWOOD CUTTINGS

PURPOSE

- Increase the presence and density of desirable woody plants
- Expand the population of a species at a particular site
- Introduce desirable species
- Eliminate handling and storage time and facilities needed for rooting plants
- Use to stabilize slopes and reduce erosion

COLLECTION SITE FOR CUTTINGS

- Site should be accessible, with reasonable population of desired plants. Owner's permission essential
- Parent plants should have vigorously growing stems and be in good health with no disease or insect infestation
- Cuttings are made with sharp tool to give smooth, clean cut

HARDWOOD CUTTINGS

- Leafless stem cuttings taken when plants are dormant
- November/December is best time
- If taken when ground is frozen, must be stored until spring

- Cuttings must have two or more nodes
- Must be kept cool and moist until 'planted'
- If storing, trim to single stem, with base of cutting clean. Bundle stems with bases all at one end, keep moist in plastic bag with peat moss and store in dark at just below 0°C

TYPES OF CUTTINGS FOR DIRECT INSERTION

- Whips are flexible, about 1 to 2 m long and 1 to 3 cm in diameter with side branches removed
- Poles are rigid and are longer and larger in diameter
- Longer cuttings can be inserted into a deeper soil layer that will be moist in summer
- Live stakes, 45 to 60 cm long

USES

- Pole cuttings can be used with rocks around plunge pools and streambanks to provide shade
- Whips can be collected in November and inserted directly into area being vegetated

SUITABLE NATIVE PLANTS

- Large willows for pole plantings
- Whips: willows, Wild Rose, Red Osier Dogwood, Meadowsweet

CUTTINGS FOR BIOTECHNICAL

PURPOSE

- To provide plant material for biotechnical and bioengineering repair work
- To identify species that will produce roots and shoots from dormant hardwood cuttings

TAKING CUTTINGS

- Select species on basis of role in bioengineering and on site conditions—See Table
- Donor site must be accessible
- Strong, healthy stems or branches
- Most require cutting when dormant (Nov. to May)
- All cuts must be clean and not crushed
- Cut bottom end on slant and top end flat
- Some applications need terminal buds and long cuttings
- Ideal to use soon after cutting
- Cuttings may be stored in ditches for a few days before installation
- Can be stored over winter if protected from drying out

The following page has a table of species that are working in Nova Scotia for slope repair.

Willow and Willow catkins

SPECIES	ROLE AND SITE	MATURE HEIGHT	COMMENTS
Pussy Willow (*Salix humilis* and *S. discolor*)	Live stakes and poles Likes moist sites	1–1.5 m	Willows are versatile Adaptable to drier sites Mature height of some may be a problem in some areas
Bebb's Willow (*Salix bebbiana*)		1–10 m; Shrub/small tree	
Red Osier Dogwood (*Cornus sericea*)	Stems and branches	1 m	Adaptable to drier sites
Meadowsweet (*Spiraea latifolia*)	Stems and branches	1 m	Adaptable to drier sites

Red Osier Dogwood

Meadowsweet

SPECIES	ROLE AND SITE	MATURE HEIGHT	COMMENTS
Red-berried Elder (*Sambucus racemosa*)	Stems and branches	3 m, but usually shorter	Adaptable to drier sites
Black-berried Elder (*Sambucus canadensis*)	Stems and branches	2–3 m	Forms large clumps, and height may be problem
Wild Rose (*Rosa virginiana*)	Stems and branches	1 m	Adaptable to drier sites
Wild Raspberry (*Rubus* spp.)	Canes, stems	1.5 m	Adaptable to drier sites Likes richer soils
Poplar (*Populus* spp.)	Stakes or poles readily root	Tree	Use only where mature height is not a problem

SUMMARY OF CONTROL TECHNIQUES

PURPOSE

- To control noxious weeds listed in the *Weed Control Act*
- To control unwanted or nuisance vegetation
- To control vegetation that interferes with safety

SELECTIVE VS. NON-SELECTIVE

- A non-selective technique controls or destroys all vegetation
- A selective technique targets a particular species or individual plant

MECHANICAL

- Mowing—timing may be critical
- Brush cutting
- Trimmers

CULTURAL

- Mulches - organic or inorganic
- Enhancing desirable vegetation
- Plant litter with allelopathic characteristics

[ABOVE] Coleophora moth used as a biological control on Sweet Clover.

BIOLOGICAL

- Organisms that target specific species or types of plants
- Insects
- Rodents and small mammals that eat tree seedlings
- Disease organisms - bacterial, fungal
- Intended release of biological control agent is covered under federal legislation: Pest Control Products Act

CHEMICAL (HERBICIDES)

- Pre-emergent, Post-emergent
- Selective herbicides kill only broad-leafed 'weeds'
- Non-selective kill all vegetation, e.g. glyphosate
- Herbicides must be registered for intended use
- Follow federal, provincial, and municipal legislation

[TOP RIGHT] Suitable site for selective control (cut stump or basal bark) of undesirable vegetation.

[FAR RIGHT] Conifer trees cutdown individually, HW 104.